JAPANESE
ETIQUETTE TODAY

JAPANE·SE ETIQUETTE TODAY

JAMES M. VARDAMAN, JR
MICHIKO SASAKI VARDAMAN

A Guide to Business
&
Social Customs

Charles E. Tuttle Company
Rutland, Vermont & Tokyo, Japan

Published by the Charles E. Tuttle Company, Inc.
of Rutland, Vermont & Tokyo, Japan
with editorial offices at
2-6 Suido 1-chome, Bunkyo-ku, Tokyo 112

© 1994 by Charles E. Tuttle Publishing Co., Inc.

LCC Card No. 93-61012
ISBN 0-8048-1933-5

First edition, 1994
Second printing, 1994

Printed in Japan

~ CONTENTS ~

~ INTRODUCTION ~

ONE CAN BECOME attuned to the different aspects of Japanese etiquette through language classes, culture classes, or living and working in Japan. With an inquiring mind, some degree of sensitivity, and the help of friends both Japanese and non-Japanese, one can learn to do things in the Japanese manner or at least recognize the proper way to do things.

Although the historical approach to etiquette and explanations of the intricacies of traditional ceremonies are of interest in themselves, in the present volume we concentrate on the etiquette of everyday life. Our premise is that although not all Japanese are polite all of the time, it makes life better for everyone when one takes the sensibilities of others into consideration. Since Japanese culture has evolved different ways of doing this than the West has, one should first become aware of the differences and then decide how much one wants to adapt. We believe that one can maintain one's own cultural identity and still develop an active awareness of Japanese-style etiquette.

In writing this volume we have operated on the assumption that a non-Japanese can, with sensitivity and some assistance, learn the everyday forms of Japanese etiquette. Often all one needs is someone to point out the proper way of doing things.

This pattern is effective up to a certain level and then other elements become necessary. The longer one lives and works in Japan and the closer a relationship one develops with Japanese people, the more apparent become certain "unspoken expectations." In the West one tends to depend on the spoken word for communication and mutual understanding. The emotive framework of Japanese society, however, is different from that of Western societies and very often Japanese do not know why they do things or why they make certain assumptions in everyday life. Unaware of precisely why they do things in a certain way, they are consequently unable to communicate the reasons in words. The "unspoken" remains that way, as does a gap between the Japanese person and the non-Japanese person.

One of the most obvious characteristics of Japanese society is its dependence on empathy in human relationships. Because a person "feels for" another person, he or she acts in a way that helps the other, often without a word being spoken. A person "reads between the lines" in conversations to find the true intent of others, imagines the emotions behind the unchanging smile of others, and in other ways pre-empts the need for verbal expression. Where a Western person might persist in asking "Why?" a Japanese person would assume that the reasons were already obvious and that verbalization was unnecessary. If words are necessary, the other person is incapable of understanding.

It is this *omoi-yari*, constantly taking others into consideration, that one cannot help admiring in Japanese society. When it is in operation, one need not express one's desires or raise one's voice in complaint. The other will already be responding to the desire or displeasure. When *omoi-yari* operates in its ultimate form, the other will tend to something before a person has even become aware of it himself or herself. Herein lies the heart of hospitality in any culture.

As we note throughout the volume, Japanese society tends to be more formal than many other societies. There is almost always a proper verbal expression for each occasion and a proper way to bow to people of each stratum of society. These patterns are acquired through a lifetime of experience. The non-Japan-born need not throw up his or her hands in resignation merely due to a late start nor assume that Japanese etiquette is a case of all or nothing. Sincerity is extremely appreciated in Japan and it can make up for an almost total ignorance of Japanese-style etiquette. If you can show that you are sincere and harbor good intentions, you can rest assured that Japanese people will respond positively to you.

CHAPTER

~ *I* ~

COMMUNICATING

~ BODY LANGUAGE ~

JAPAN HAS a culture which values self-restraint, consideration for others, humility, and formality. Naturally these values affect how Japanese feel one should carry oneself, so let us consider a few general rules.

In conversations it is considered poor manners to leave one's hands in one's pockets, stand with one leg crossed over the other, lean against a wall or door, or chew gum. When seated, Japanese may cross their legs at the ankles or knees, but generally consider the ankle-over-the-knee cross too informal even for men. It is not considered proper to stick one's legs out in front of one either on tatami or in a chair. When one encounters a low sofa, if one wishes to show respect for the other party, one will not lean back, but rather sit forward on the edge.

When sitting on tatami, men will often start out sitting on their legs out of politeness, then later shift to the less formal cross-legged position. Women will start out sitting on their legs, then may later tuck their legs to one side. It would be most improper for a woman to sit cross-legged in polite company.

It is considered impolite to blow one's nose in public. Paper tissues are used for doing the job quietly and are then discarded. The handkerchief is for wiping the mouth, removing sweat from the face, or wiping the hands when leaving the washroom.

Although Japanese self-expression in its nonverbal

form tends to be restrained, this does not mean that self-expression does not exist. As a case in point, Japanese smile to communicate anger, happiness, confusion, embarrassment, sadness, and disappointment. With a minimum of sensitivity it is possible to discern the emotion behind the smile. When one goes beyond merely "reading" the facial expression, one can recognize a broad range of emotions being expressed. One emotion that Japanese tend not to express in public is affection. Young people will walk arm in arm and occasionally kiss in public, but this is considered improper behavior.

The same self-restraint is apparent in verbal components of expression, and to avoid seeming unpleasantly aggressive or assertive it is important to avoid excessively demonstrative gesturing, displays of displeasure, and loud speech. This is not to suggest that one must adopt the Japanese style completely, but it is to one's advantage to tone down the vigor and dimension of physical expressiveness and the volume of verbal expressiveness. Especially in public places such as trains and buses, it is important to avoid overextending one's self as a result of loud speech, spreading out in seats, and broad gesturing. Public transportation is crowded enough as it is, without people monopolizing space or speaking loud enough for everyone in the vehicle to follow a conversation.

One rarely finds oneself in a situation where the de facto Japanese national anthem, "Kimigayo," is played, but on such occasions as the final day of a sumo tournament a non-Japanese will be properly respectful by standing silently while the song is played or sung.

~ BOWING ~

BOWING IS the most important of all Japanese forms of nonverbal communication to master. In the West, bowing is often seen as an expression of subservience, but in Japanese society the bow is an expression of respect for others and personal humility. It may also be used as a greeting or to express gratitude. Hence, it is important to avoid being overly casual with a mere nod of the head or unknowingly rude by making an exaggeratedly deep bow when it is not called for.

When two Japanese people are introduced to one another by a mutual acquaintance, the friendliness they show and the kind of bow they make will be determined by their relations to the common friend. To honor their friend, they will be polite to the unknown person. When two Japanese men meet for the first time without the assistance of a mutual friend, they will generally make a perfunctory first bow because they do not yet know how they rank in relation to one another. Once they exchange name cards and carefully read the other's card, they will then make the appropriate bow and greeting. A president of a large corporation would seem foolish if he bowed deeply to a clerk of a small shop, and the clerk would be greatly embarrassed as well. This does not mean that the two are not equal as human beings, but their social status is clearly different.

Non-Japanese need not be overly concerned about the finest intricacies of rank, but it is important to show generally appropriate consideration for others during introductions, greetings, and farewells. Proper manners when one is standing call for an informal bow of about fifteen degrees for casual occasions between people of all ranks. A more formal bow of thirty degrees is used toward seniors in rank. It is important in bowing to keep the feet together, the back straight, and the hands at the side. In the most formal bow of forty-five degrees or more, one should place the palms of the hands on the front of one's legs.

Sales clerks in department stores where employees are properly trained will bow thirty degrees as a greeting and forty-five degrees or more as an expression of gratitude to a customer who has made a purchase. In such a situation, the customer merely nods in acknowledgment. One also nods casually to waiters and cashiers.

When one is in a Western-style room, two parties will stand and bow during introductions and the exchange of name cards; however, formal greetings in tatami rooms are more intricate. When one is paying a

16

Most formal bow   Semiformal bow   Informal bow

visit to someone's home, the greetings in the entrance (*genkan*) are temporary greetings which may be followed later by more formal greetings inside the house. Before sitting on a cushion (*zabuton*) in a tatami room, one should sit on one's knees on the tatami, look at the other person, and bow from the waist. In the ordinary bow one places one's hands in front of one's knees and leans forward so that the fingertips touch the tatami. In the formal bow one places one's hands flat on the tatami, forming a ninety-degree angle, and bows until one's head touches one's hands. Women place their hands so that their fingertips touch and men keep their hands two to four inches apart. Once the formalities are complete, then one may sit on the offered sitting cushion.

When greeting non-Japanese, Japanese men have also adopted the practice of shaking hands, often with a light grip and an accompanying nod of the head. Some men even use the firm grip and direct eye contact of the West. In general, however, when you

Formal bow

Ordinary bow

shake hands, avoid gripping unnecessarily firmly, coming too close to the other person, and backslapping. Japanese women have in general not adopted the custom of shaking hands, so bowing is still the accepted greeting.

When one presents or accepts a gift, it is considered humble and appreciative to use both hands. Both parties should also make an appropriate bow. Gifts are to be accepted and then placed to one side. Unless one is specifically urged to open the gift right then and there, it is polite to wait until later and open it in private.

~ GESTURES ~

IT IS BEYOND the purview of this volume to introduce the whole range of Japanese gestures, but there are a few that specifically involve manners.

The Japanese nod to show attentiveness and agreement, but they do not employ a shake of the head to signal no. Instead, they hold the hand flat in front of their face and wave it back and forth. This gesture can indicate disagreement, denial, lack of understanding, or humility in response to a compliment.

The gesture that signifies oneself is a forefinger pointed to one's nose. Since it is impolite to point at others, one may indicate you or the other person with the hand palm up and fingers together in the direction of the referent.

When cutting in front of someone, in a crowded area, for example, one holds the hand straight out like

"No."

"Me."

a tennis racket and with a slight chopping motion indicates that one would like to be excused for rudely walking in front. In a theater, stadium, or situation where you must pass in front of others in a row to take your own seat, you may bow and use the chopping gesture as you move in front of those who are already seated. As you pass down the row, turn your back to the people in the row.

The gesture for beckoning someone is the hand extended forward palm down and the fingers making a waving motion.

The thumb and forefinger holding an imaginary

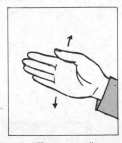

"Excuse me."

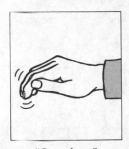

"Come here."

"How about a drink?"

20

saké cup and tossing it back is the gesture for drinking, as in an invitation to go drinking.

The illustrations of the hands indicate the Japanese method of counting from one to ten on one hand. First, one folds the thumb into the palm for number one. Numbers two through five are indicated by bending the index finger, then the middle finger, etc., over the thumb. One then reverses the process to signify numbers six through ten by straightening one finger at a time, beginning with the little finger. This way of counting is generally only used when counting to oneself. Although it is not

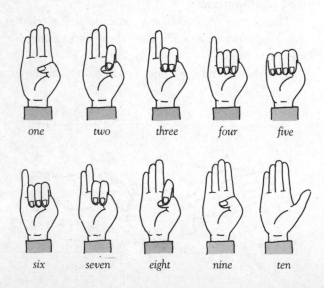

one   two   three   four   five

six   seven   eight   nine   ten

used in polite company, the gesture for six with the hand turned outward also means woman or girl-friend.

It is considered polite for a woman to place one hand in front of her mouth when she laughs, as it is impolite to show one's teeth.

Further information on gestures and body language will be found throughout this volume, especially in the section on eating and drinking.

~ VERBAL EXPRESSION ~

WITH REGARD to the verbal components of Japanese, it is important to note that the Japanese language generally requires frequent use of rejoinders (*aizuchi*), words or sounds that indicate the listener is following the speaker. The short words *ee*, *hai*, and *sō* (*desu*) *ne* are inserted in conversation to show attentiveness, if not agreement. It is a mistake to assume that *hai* (usually understood as yes) means agreement. In many contexts all it means is that the listener is paying attention to what the speaker is saying. In face-to-face conversation, a nod of the head can communicate the same thing, but telephone conversations require an occasional rejoinder to reassure the other party that one is still on the line.

CHAPTER

~ *II* ~

INTRODUCTIONS

~ JAPANESE NAMES ~

FIRST OF ALL, we should note that Japanese family names precede personal names, so it is not helpful to refer to first or last names. Suzuki Kazuo-san becomes in English Mr. Kazuo Suzuki, and Takahashi Yuriko-san becomes Ms. Yuriko Takahashi. When Japanese write their own names in English, it is up to them to decide which name order to follow.

In normal day-to-day relationships, Japanese call one another by their family names, no matter how long they may have known each other. Children—and adult friends who have known each other since child-hood—may use personal names (Kazuo-san and Yuriko-san), special nicknames, or diminutives (for example, Yuriko becoming Yuri-chan), but as a departure point one generally sticks with the family name plus -san.

Still, there should be no rush on either side of a cross-cultural relationship to start using personal names as a sign of friendship. If the Japanese friend or associate suggests it, then follow suit, but one should not make a Japanese person feel uncomfortable by insisting on using personal names. It is especially uncomfortable in groups if you call one person Kazuo and another person Nakamura-san. Closeness of rela-tionship need not always be expressed verbally in public. Finally, be aware that in Japanese it is impolite to drop the -san from another person's name.

There are times when you should use a person's title or position name rather than the family name. Medical doctors and teachers of whatever rank or prestige are called *sensei*. If a man named Tanaka is a tea-ceremony instructor, university professor, or brain surgeon, you should call him *sensei* or Tanaka *sensei* but never Tanaka-san.

In the business world you will also hear the titles *shachō* (president of a company), *buchō* (department head), *kachō* (section head), and *kakarichō* (head clerk). In some companies these titles are used as forms of address or in reference to third parties, always without -san. In other companies everyone from top to bottom is called by family name followed by -san. When in doubt, you will not be considered rude if you follow the latter custom.

~ INTRODUCTIONS ~

WHEN MEETING Japanese for the first time you should remember several important things. First of all, if you are unable to function in Japanese, the other person will be forced to use a foreign language. It may well be that the person you are meeting has spent twenty years abroad and is fluent in five languages, but it may also be that the person has not spoken English for twenty years. You can make up for your lack of language proficiency by either memorizing how to say "John Smith *desu. Dōzo yoroshiku o-negai shimasu*" or carefully enunciating "My name is John Smith. I'm happy to meet you." Speaking clearly is polite, but speaking very slowly or in a loud voice is plainly condescending.

It is always entertaining to see a non-Japanese man bow at the exact moment that a Japanese man extends his hand to shake hands, each person attempting to be considerate of the other. You might start with a polite bow to show consideration for Japanese custom, but play it by ear and be prepared to shake. For the finer points of bowing, refer to page 15.

~ NAME CARDS ~

THE KEY ELEMENT in the use of names and introductions is the business card or name card (meishi). It would be odd for the average college student or housewife to carry name cards, but virtually everyone who is gainfully employed or has some affiliation with an organization carries them. Unless you are a tourist, it is helpful to have some kind of business card to hand out when you meet people. The usual format, as shown in the illustrations, has English on one side and Japanese on the reverse. Both sides should have your name, the name of the organization with which you are affiliated, your position within that organization (your katagaki), and the organization's address and telephone number. It certainly creates a better impression at an initial meeting if you have a nicely printed card to exchange with the people you meet. Cards are neither heavy to carry nor terribly expensive to have printed, and they provide a clear identification. The people you

MARY G. SMITH

Director of Sales
ABC, Incorporated

1-2-3 Suido
Bunkyo-ku, Tokyo 112
(03) 3123-4567

1234 Broadway
New York, NY 10019
(212) 725-9876

meet will find it easier to remember your name, which is as foreign to them as Japanese names may be to you, and they will know exactly how to contact you later should that be necessary.

Having a card printed in English only is better than nothing, but having

ＡＢＣ株式会社
販売部

部長

メリー・Ｇ・スミス

〒112
東京都文京区水道一丁目二ー三
ＴＥＬ
（〇三）
三一二三ー四五六七

the Japanese in addition will make it much easier for the other person to read and remember. In Japan, business cards are usually printed in lots of one hundred, the first hundred going for about four thousand yen for two-sided printing.

There are many kinds of leather, plastic, even metal card cases to put your cards in. Rather than stuffing your own cards and the cards you receive in a shirt or blouse pocket, it is more polite and business-like to carry them in a functional case in the inside pocket of a suit or in a handbag.

The proper manner for exchanging cards during introductions is to remove a card from its case and turn it so that the other person can read the Japanese side as you hand it to him or her. Hold the card in the top left corner grasped between the thumb and index finger of the right hand, extend it toward the other person, and simultaneously bow as you introduce yourself verbally. To be very polite, you hold the top corners of the card between the thumb and forefinger of both hands.

Bow slightly as you receive the other person's card between your thumb and forefinger. Once you have the card, read it carefully. It is acceptable to confirm verbally how to pronounce the person's name. Once you have grasped the person's name, position, and organization, bow once more in accordance with the degree of deference you think appropriate. Once you have done this, slip the card into a separate section of your card case. It is also acceptable once the introductions are completed to place the other person's card on the table in front of you and leave it there during the conversation. However, it is impolite to write on another person's card in his or her presence, so if you wish to make a notation, do it afterward.

Stationery stores sell name-card albums (*meishi horudā*) that are very convenient for arranging the cards you collect. Your card will end up in another person's collection, so be sure that the information on the card is current.

~ CONVERSATIONAL ~ CONSIDERATIONS

30   IF THE TWO parties in a conversation are equally fluent in Japanese and English, use the language of the person higher in rank. If there is no difference in status, you might also use the other person's mother tongue out of courtesy. In business, it is common sense to use the language of the client. In a group where not everyone is bilingual, try to avoid leaving anyone entirely out of the conversation, because it is terribly boring to "watch" a conversation for any length of time.

When speaking a foreign language, a person may adopt the conventions of that language or maintain the conventions of his or her mother tongue. A Japanese person may become more direct or aggressive when using English, thinking that this is the custom of English speakers. Another Japanese speaker may seem excessively polite and self-effacing in English by virtue of having translated directly into English the traditional Japanese manners of speech. To avoid misunderstandings it is important to keep in mind that the language spoken is not always the language in which a thought was conceived. This goes for a native English speaker attempting to communicate in Japanese and for the native Japanese speaker trying to communicate in English.

When you rely on English, you should be conscious that you are asking the other party to carry more weight in a conversation. You can lighten that burden by speaking a bit more slowly, more concisely, and more clearly than you would normally. Even if a Japanese speaks English with apparent ease, idiomatic expressions, slang, and colloquialisms are difficult to grasp, so try to limit use of them. Also, remember that humor is usually culture-bound and that even if the Japanese person understands the vocabulary you use, the punch line may lose its impact in another culture. Should you be fortunate enough to have an interpreter, make his or her job easier by sticking to basics.

When you are able to use Japanese, remember the importance of choosing the appropriate level of politeness to suit the occasion and the people involved. Addressing an older person in the same language you use with close Japanese friends is a definite faux pas.

Good listeners are especially appreciated in Japan and this means that it is better not to be too talkative, or not to interrupt or finish another person's sentence, but rather to indicate at intervals that you are interested in what the other person is saying. It is important to occasionally nod your head and use *aizuchi* such as *ee, ah sō desu ka, hai,* and *naruhodo* when you speak Japanese, and "uh-huh," "hmm," "I see," etc., when speaking in English.

Though we prefer not to spend too much time discussing the Japanese language, mention should be made of several expressions that relate to manners. *Yoroshiku* is used when one wants to ask for another person's future favors, especially in an informal introduction. *Yoroshiku o-negai shimasu* is a more formal expression that is used to ask the other party to show you general kindnesses or do you a specific favor. It is often used in a very ambiguous way when one is asking for favorable treatment in general. *Okagesama de* is a way of expressing gratitude to the other person for inquiring about your family, your health, or your progress in some project. It means literally "thanks to you," but it is used even when the other person has absolutely nothing to do with the event or person being inquired about. It comes from a larger world view that holds that everyone is responsible in some distant way for the good things that one experiences. *O-sewasama* is a way of thanking someone for doing something, from delivering the mail to your home to far more significant services. *O-negai shimasu* is an expression one uses to ask a favor, either very specific or very general in nature.

~ GIFTS ~

AS WE DISCUSS in detail in the sections on gift giving, it is polite to bring gifts to people that you already know or who you are planning to meet for the first time. It is not necessary to bring little things for people who will serve you, such as maids or waiters, but it is highly recommended that you select something that is of good quality and easy to carry for people you will be staying with, people you will visit on business, and others who will be helping you in major ways.

Avoid things that are marked "Made in Japan," and remember that however simple the gift may be, it will always appear better if it is nicely wrapped and not simply presented in a wrinkled, brown paper bag.

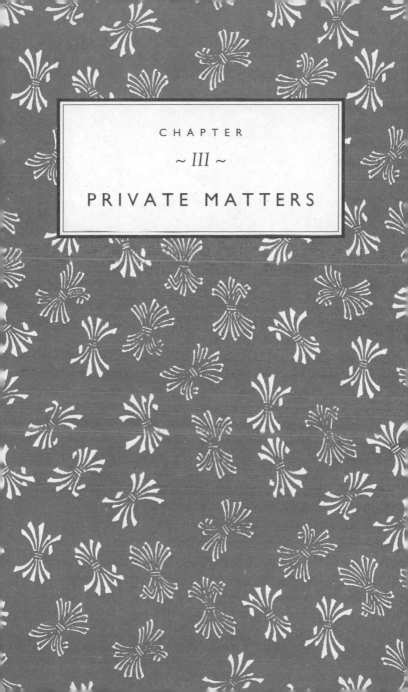

CHAPTER

~ *III* ~

PRIVATE MATTERS

~ CLOTHING ~

ALTHOUGH JAPANESE are becoming slightly more casual, they continue to be rather more careful about the way they dress than people from other countries. Therefore, when you are planning the wardrobe you will wear in Japan, it is wise to plan to be just one level dressier than you might be in your home country. People will form an impression from the way you dress, so it is to your advantage to have nice-looking clothes, even if they are casual.

In Japan you will have many occasions for removing footwear and putting on slippers inside homes and in Japanese inns and restaurants, so it is highly recommended that you bring at least one pair of shoes which do not have to be tied and that you leave at home boots that require elaborate lacing. It is awkward, to say the least, to have to tie and untie footwear in narrow spaces where other people are standing by waiting for you. It is much easier to use the long-handled shoehorns that are provided and slip gracefully into no-tie shoes. This holds true for both men and women.

~ BATHING ~

BY TRADITION the bathing facilities and the toilet are in separate rooms in Japan. They may be next to one another, but they are not in the same room, except in Western-style houses and hotels where tradition surrenders to economy of space.

In private homes the bathing facilities are usually composed of two rooms, an anteroom with a sink and a mirror where one changes clothes, and the room where the actual bath is. In most situations one locks the door between the anteroom and the outside corridor to make sure others know the bath is in use. Except among family members, it is not proper for one person to use the sink while someone else is using the bath, even if the rooms are separate. In this anteroom one removes all of one's clothing and carefully folds and piles it either on the counter or in the basket that may be provided for this purpose.

You leave the bath towel in the anteroom and take the washcloth (*tenugui*) with you into the bath and close the door. The tub may be covered with boards or some kind of rolling cover to keep the water hot, so first remove that and set it aside. You will probably find a small scoop, a bowl, and a low stool. The scoop is for stirring the water in the tub, which is hotter on the surface, and taking water from the tub for washing. The bowl is for washing yourself.

Bathing is generally a three-part exercise. First rinse briefly and enter the tub to warm up. Then get out, sit on the stool, scrub yourself using water in the bowl, and rinse thoroughly. Finally relax in the tub again. All of the soaping and shampooing takes place outside of the tub with water from the shower head (if there is one), the spigot, or the tub itself. Do not take too much water out of the tub because the person who follows you will not have enough. It is important to remember that the tub water is communal—everyone in the family uses the same hot water to relax in. Therefore, you should not scrub yourself in the tub or get dirt or soapsuds in it. Also, do not empty the tub when you are finished.

When you complete your bath and rinse off, rinse off the stool, scoop, and bowl and return them to where they were and cover the tub again. After a first drying off with the washcloth, go back to the anteroom and dry off completely with the other towel. When you are through, fold both towels and leave them on the counter.

Bathing at a public bath (*sentō*) is quite similar to the process described above, but there are a few variations. For the uninitiated, it should be noted that this "communal bath" has separate entrances and separate facilities for the two sexes. The only "connection" is the proprietor's booth, which sits astride the partition between the two sides of the changing room. You may purchase or borrow for a fee everything for taking a bath at this booth, but usually customers bring in their own bowl or bag the necessary shampoo, rinse, soap, towels, comb, and brush. Find an empty locker, place your clothing inside, and remove the key. From this large changing room you go into the large bathroom and find a vacant stool and spigot. Wash off the stool, sit down, and rinse yourself off. Once you are superficially clean, you can warm up in one of the tubs. Although not everyone follows the rules, you should not take your washcloth into the tub, but leave it on the edge of the bath or in your bowl.

Once you are warm, get out, scrub down, rinse off, then get back in for a longer soak. When finished, place the stool back under the spigot, and return to the changing rooms. The older generation may be a little less conscious of nakedness than the younger generation, but no one makes much to-do about being seen undressed.

38

Many Japanese-style inns offer baths fed by natural hot springs (*onsen*) and they are similar to public baths, except that in some the water has such a high natural mineral content (sulphur, for example) that soap and shampoo will not lather and may even be prohibited. Because of the mineral content it is recommended to leave all jewelry behind in your room.

~ TOILETS ~

SINCE MANY public toilets provide neither towels for drying hands nor toilet paper, it is wise to always carry a handkerchief for the former purpose and a small pack of tissues for the latter. Toilets on trains and in train stations are among the least pleasant; those in department stores are much better.

Although Western-style toilets continue to increase, there are occasions when only Japanese-style facilities are available. One takes care of one's business by squatting astride the toilet, facing the raised end.

In private homes, inns, and some public facilities, slippers or sandals are provided inside the entrance of the restroom, so be sure to change footwear on the way in and again on the way out.

Japanese toilet stalls are enclosed all the way to the floor, so it is not possible to quickly ascertain whether the stall is occupied. The Japanese custom is to knock on the door. If there is no answering knock from the inside, then open the door. It is not polite to straight-away pull on the knob. Nor is it necessary to verbally announce that someone is inside the stall; a return knock efficiently conveys that message.

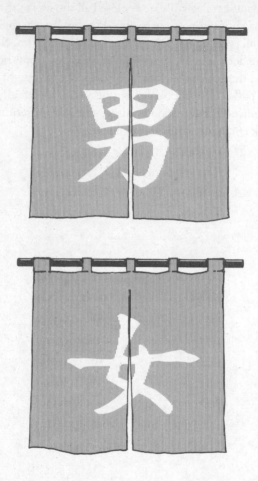

Curtains are hung at the entrance to the bath in a hotel or inn.
The character on the top curtain indicates the men's bath, and
the one on the bottom the women's bath.

CHAPTER

~ *IV* ~

HOMES

~ TAKING UP RESIDENCE ~

IF YOU HAVE made the decision to settle in for a while,
unless you remain in a foreign enclave, you will want
to follow Japanese customs vis-à-vis your neighbors.
Moving in can be a rather hectic experience, so you
may want to spend the first few days in your new place
just unpacking and locating things. But within the first
two or three days of your move it is highly recommended that you pay courtesy calls on your neighbors.

Such visits are not mandatory, but you will rarely
have as good an opportunity to meet your immediate
neighbors, learn about the area, and garner goodwill.
Since your neighbors may not know quite what to
make of you, by making the first move through this
widely accepted custom, you will not only be able to
meet everyone immediately but also pave the way for
getting essential information about garbage collection
and local customs. With minor expenditures of time
and money you will be able to show goodwill in a way
that will never come again.

In a residential neighborhood, it is standard to visit
the house on either side of yours and the three houses
opposite. In apartments and condominiums, if your
apartment is in the middle of a floor of apartments,
then visiting the two next-door neighbors is generally
sufficient. If your apartment is one of four or six in the
same stairwell, then you will probably meet all of the

residents in the normal comings and goings, so it is best to call on all of them.

Usually new residents take a small gift such as a towel or soap (approximately five hundred yen) and introduce themselves as the people next door. If you have a small family, it would be nice if everyone were to go; if your family is large or one spouse is particularly busy, then the other spouse can act as representative for everyone. The best time to visit is in early evening after dinner or on the weekend. Long conversation is not expected, so you can just introduce yourself and tell who the members of your family are (whether they are present or not), hand your neighbor your business card if you have one, smile, and ask for their future kindnesses (*Dōzo yoroshiku o-negai shimasu*).

There are several minor neighborly duties that everyone is expected to perform. To keep the neighborhood looking nice, it is each family's duty to sweep the road in front of their house. You needn't do this three times a day, but if some thoughtless person drops trash in front of your house, it is best not to wait for someone else to pick it up.

The regular garbage pickups are generally followed by a neighbor cleaning up the collection spot with a broom and dustpan. This duty rotates through the neighborhood, so smile when it's your turn. It is not a long-term burden and everyone benefits from a cleaner neighborhood.

The local neighborhood association (*chōnaikai*) representative will probably call on you shortly after you move in to welcome you to the neighborhood and to collect a small membership fee (usually three to five hundred yen for three months) for association activities. Everyone in the neighborhood benefits in some small way, so smile, pay the minimal sum, and trust that it will be used to good ends. In all likelihood you will receive a newsletter from the association that announces major neighborhood events such as fire drills, power shortages, and changes in garbage-collection days. There may also be a collection for local Red Cross activities. The representatives are volunteers and they are contributing their time to making the neighborhood a nice place to live, so your financial contribution is a normal part of belonging to the neighborhood. Whenever they call on you, respond with a hearty *O-sewasama desu*.

When you move out of your neighborhood, it is polite to call on the same neighbors as you did when you moved in and perhaps offer them another small gift, such as a towel. This is an opportunity to inform your neighbors of what is happening to your residence, thank them for their help over the years, and tell them your forwarding address, if you care to.

~ VISITING OTHERS ~ AT HOME

WHEN CALLING on others in the cooler months one is usually wearing a coat. Traditional etiquette says that before you announce yourself you should remove your coat, but there is a newer view that such an action implies that you are prepared to enter the house and stay for a while. That would, of course, be presumptuous, so what should one do? If you are a guest who has been invited, it is best to remove your coat, muffler, hat, and gloves before ringing the doorbell. If you are unexpected or if you are calling for brief business, then it is best to leave your coat on.

Rude delivery men will still open the front door of a house and call out to the occupant in lieu of ringing the doorbell, but this custom is fortunately disappearing. When visiting a home, you commence with the doorbell or a knock on the door and say *Gomen kudasai*. When someone appears at the door, you commence with a bow. If you are expected, the host or hostess will invite you to come in with several repetitions of *Dōzo*. It is not that the person thinks you did not hear correctly the first time. It is simply considered polite to repeat invitations.

Though Japanese houses have become less traditional and more compact over the years, there is still a *genkan* (ground-level floor area) just inside the front door. It is here that you slip out of your outside footwear, step up into the house proper, and put on slippers. Before you step up, it is polite to say *O-jama shimasu*.

Shoes with laces make the above maneuver more difficult, so loafers or other slip-on shoes are the preferred footwear. You will notice that even when Japanese men wear laced shoes, the shoes are often left tied. Men slip in and out of them without touching the laces by using a long-handled shoehorn. It does not look very nice, but if you must, sit down on the step to remove your shoes. At all costs, avoid stepping in your stockinged feet on the floor of the *genkan*. If you step there and then step up into the house, you will, in effect, be bringing in dirt. To be proper, one steps up into the house, then turns and arranges one's shoes so that they are off to one side and with the toes pointing toward the exit. Should a guest not do this, the correct host or hostess will at some time during the visit arrange the shoes so that the guest can more easily slip into them upon leaving.

When you are either receiving visitors at your home

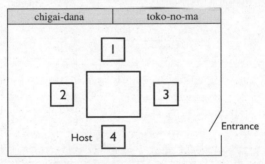

Seating order in a Japanese-style (tatami) room

or paying a formal visit to someone else's home, for example at New Year's, you will want to be aware of the seating preferences shown in the illustration, in which position one is for the most honored.

What do you do when the Japanese-style room has no *toko-no-ma* (alcove)? Keep in mind these consider-ations: (1) The seat of honor is on the right as you enter. (2) The seat of honor is farthest from the door. (3) The seat of honor has the best view of the garden or window.

A kind host or hostess will show the guest to the room and indicate exactly where the person is to be seated. If one is not shown where to sit and is left to await the return of the host or hostess, one should temporarily take the seat closest to the door, the seat considered "lowest" in the room. Upon return, the host or hostess will in a flurry indicate that the guest should take the seat of honor. It is impolite to assume that you are honored and plunk down in the seat of honor uninvited.

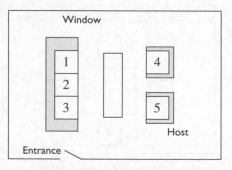

Seating order in a Western-style room

In a tatami room there will be cushions for each person to sit on. One performs polite, formal greetings seated on tatami, as indicated in the section on bowing, then slips onto the cushion. The polite way is to sit on your heels. Even if you cannot survive that way for long, make the effort to show that you know the proper etiquette. In all likelihood, the host or hostess will see your anguish and suggest that you sit more comfortably. Women may shift their legs to one side; men may cross their legs. It is rude to stick your legs out in front of youself, so avoid that at all costs unless you have a particular problem bending your knees.

If there is a table with an electric heating unit underneath (*denki-gotatsu*) or a traditional sunken area covered with a table (*hori-gotatsu*), you can stick your knees or legs under the blanket covering the table frame in order to get warm. The *hori-gotatsu*, rare in the modern age, is especially welcome because you can put your feet down in the compartment below the table and sit on the *zabuton* as if you were in a chair. More likely you will be in an electric *kotatsu* seated on your heels or cross-legged.

Although in some countries the kitchen is the site of friendly conversation, in Japan the kitchen has traditionally been off-limits to males and visitors. Whatever the reasons for this, do not wander in uninvited. Guests also do not volunteer to wash dishes or clean off the table after a meal. Young people may be less adamant about this and may even appreciate the help, but the rule stands that the host or hostess should not allow the guest to do such things. It is considered disrespectful to the guest to allow such assistance and disrespectful to the host or hostess to suggest it.

When one uses the toilet facilities, one will find a pair of slippers for the exclusive use of that one small room. Leave your house slippers outside the toilet door—partially to indicate that the facilities are in use—and slip on the special pair on the other side of the threshold. Once you have finished, be sure to leave the toilet pair inside turned the way you found them and slip into the house slippers again. All of this changing of footwear may seem troublesome, but the Japanese prefer to maintain clear distinctions between areas with different degrees of cleanliness.

If a guest is invited beforehand to stay overnight, he or she will probably have brought a gift of fruit or flowers at the very least and probably some nightwear and a toothbrush. At bathtime the guest is invited to go first. In some cases the whole family will be waiting for the guest to finish, so the guest should not stall for whatever reason once the invitation is given. A short-term visitor may play the guest and contribute nothing to the household, but a longer-term guest may try to treat the hosts to dinner out or in another way show appreciation. Generally the lady of the house will offer to do laundry for guests.

Japanese families use set expressions when they come and go and a house guest will want to follow suit. Upon leaving one says *Itte kimasu* or *Itte mairimasu* and the person who is sending off says *Itte irasshai*. When one returns to the house one says *Tadaima* and the person greeting says *O-kaeri nasai*. These expressions are also used in Japanese inns, although the innkeeper may also use more polite expressions because you are the guest. In many offices the same expressions are used among colleagues as they come and go during the business day.

Hospitality in Japanese homes inevitably involves serving tea or meals. The illustrations show the proper placement of tea, cake, and a small damp towel (*o-shibori*) for the guest to wipe his hands with before eating, and the proper order for serving guests. Serving

Tea, cake, and o-shibori

commences with the person farthest from the door, then follows the order indicated. For the arrangement of Japanese meals on trays (*o-zen*) or tables, see the illustration on page 70.

It should be noted that it is polite for hostesses and hosts to continue offering guests food and drink and for the guests to accept the hospitality with moderation. One need not endlessly push food and beverage on a

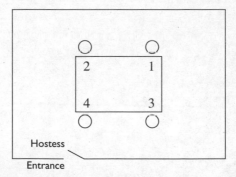

Serving order in a Western-style room

guest nor consume every morsel that is offered. What is important is that the hostess or host has made every effort to show hospitality and that the guest shows appreciation for the efforts made. It is not rude to say that you have thoroughly enjoyed what you have eaten and that you think you have had enough but thanks anyway.

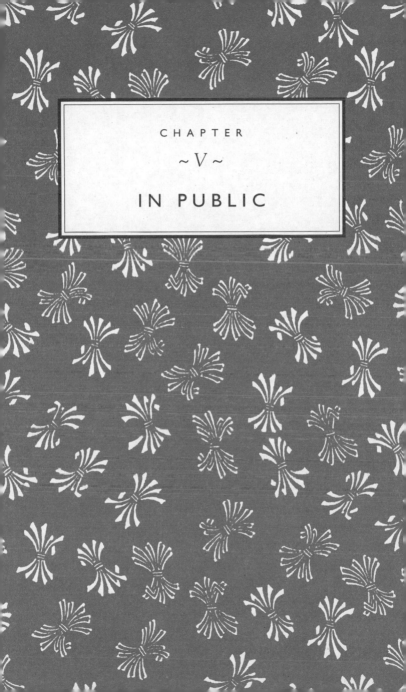

CHAPTER

~ V ~

IN PUBLIC

~ ON THE MOVE ~

IF A TAXI is available for a fare, a simple wave of the hand will be sufficient to flag it down. No one whistles or shouts. Once a taxi pulls over, remember the golden rule of taxis: never touch the door handle. The driver has a remote-control device that opens and closes the left rear door for the passenger. The driver will open it for you to get in and close it once you are safely inside. If there is not enough room in the back seat and you must sit in the front passenger seat, you will have to open that door yourself. For safety reasons, everyone in the back seat should enter by the left door. Once you reach your destination, pay the fare (no tipping necessary or expected), collect the receipt if you need it, and let the driver tend to the left rear door again.

Just as there are hierarchies of seating inside a home or office, there is a proper order for automobiles. There are overriding considerations such as luggage or lack of mobility, but the illustrations show the proper order,

55

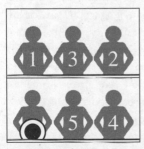

Seating order in a taxi

Seating order in a private car

with position one being reserved for the most honored, to a maximum of five passengers.

While we are on the subject of vehicles, we should note that on trains and planes the order of respect is window seat, then aisle seat, and middle seat last. Since personal preference may vary, the most honored person should be allowed to choose first.

~ TRAVELING ~

JAPAN IS the land of commemorative photographs (*kinen shashin*), so if you are traveling with Japanese companions you will garner goodwill if you offer to take everyone's picture occasionally. Later you can have copies made and send or hand-deliver them to your fellow travelers. You need not be professional, because the thought is what counts. Needless to say, put the photos in envelopes and when you present them, politely but firmly refuse any payment for the cost.

One of the great pleasures of Japanese train or bus travel is eating. In every major station and terminal you will find boxed lunches (*bentō*) to take on board. In many long-distance trains, carts of similar lunches are available, but you have a better selection in the stations. Japanese, with the exception of business people, often bring additional food from home for others in their party to share. Food that is already divided into portions and can be easily eaten on a moving train is preferable. Note that with a disposable lunch box Japanese tie the empty box up neatly before disposing of it. Also, Japanese tend not to eat while they are walking or while they are traveling on commuter trains and subways.

If your travel plans include an overnight stay in a Japanese-style inn (*ryokan*), "people's lodging" (*minshuku*), or pension, you should take your own bath towels with you, because generally they are not provided. Large places may have rooms with a bath, but the general arrangement is large communal baths, either separate ones for men and women or separate ones for the guests to use room by room. You need to look presentable as you walk down the hallway between your room and the bath, something to consider in your selection of clothing for the trip. When informal cotton kimono (*yukata*) are provided, you may use them for going to the bath. The left side should go over the right side of the *yukata*. Men tie theirs on the hip at the back and women tie theirs at the waist on the right side.

~ TEMPLES AND ~ SHRINES

WHEN YOU VISIT temples and shrines, watching the behavior of others will be your most helpful clue as to what is and is not acceptable. There will be a large wooden offertory box with bars across the top for visitors to drop coins in. You are under no obligation to contribute, but dropping in a few spare coins would not be rude.

As a general rule one does not step up into the sanctuary of such buildings. Worshippers will usually stand outside an obvious barrier and make their obeisances there. If the sanctuary is open to the public, people will generally be expected to remove their shoes before entering. If there are no people present for you to imitate, it is better not to walk in.

Occasionally there are private ceremonies and services being held inside the sanctuary, so refrain from loud noises and photography in deference.

58

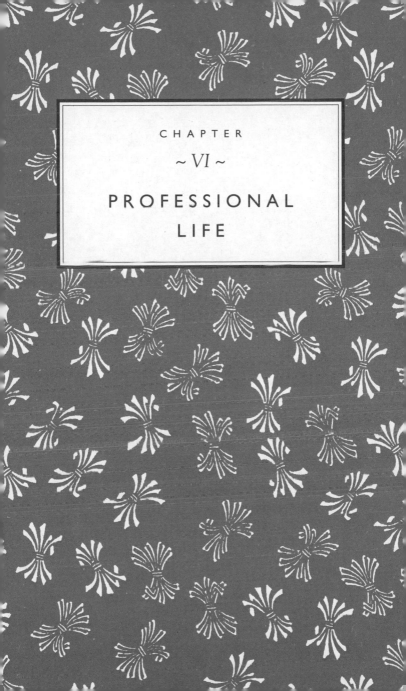

CHAPTER

~ VI ~

PROFESSIONAL
LIFE

THE JAPANESE tendency toward formality is obvious in the business world. First-rate companies teach new employees how to do everything from answering the telephone to exchanging name cards. From a Western point of view well-trained employees may seem stiff, but they are exhibiting the proper manners that keep a company's image sparkling.

A second characteristic of the business world as a whole is that things tend to move slowly. From one perspective carrying on irrelevant conversation and holding endless meetings over cups of tea is a waste of time. From another perspective this sort of casual discussion is an important preface to decision making, and through the exchange of information and opinion one learns whom one is dealing with. Investing a little time and effort shows a willingness to cooperate according to accepted practice and a commitment to the long run. A person who is pushy, irritable, and demanding will find this slowness exasperating and will probably do poorly in Japanese circles. A person who can sip tea contentedly and participate in the give-and-take will make use of such occasions to invest in long-term relationships.

~ IMPORTANT RULES OF ~ OFFICE ETIQUETTE

62

NATURALLY AT the beginning of each workday one should greet the others in one's office, each with the appropriate level of politeness. During the day when one encounters these same colleagues in an office corridor, one should acknowledge them again. Depending on who the other person is, one may merely nod in passing or, to be most polite, come to a complete stop, greet the other person with a bow, and wait politely until the other person has passed before proceeding on one's way.

At the end of the work day, one excuses oneself for preceding others out of the office by saying *O-saki ni shitsurei shimasu*. The one who remains may say *Gokurōsama* to a subordinate or colleague for work that has been appreciated even if expected. Others may say *O-tsukaresama* at the end of the day.

Japanese society depends heavily on connections and it is extremely difficult in ordinary business life to obtain an appointment with busy people by simply calling up, introducing yourself, and asking to see the person in charge. That is simply not how the game is played. You have a much greater chance of success if you can arrange an introduction through someone who is already connected with the party you wish to meet. This network of relationships takes time and effort to cultivate, but it is the sine qua non of professional life. It is built up over a long period of time spent drinking tea and beer with a variety of people.

Before calling on a contact, one should call ahead to request an appointment at the other person's convenience. Simply dropping by, unless it is to pick up a pamphlet or something, is impolite and unprofessional. Needless to say, it is proper to appear on time for all appointments. If you are unavoidably delayed, phone ahead or en route to apologize for the delay and inquire if a postponement of some length is possible. One simply does not appear late without making prior efforts to make contact.

The first person you will encounter in an office will be a receptionist. If you are calling at the office for the first time, as you introduce yourself verbally you may also wish to present a name card to be sure the person knows who you are. Tell the receptionist whom you have an appointment with, then wait for the message to be conveyed. In all likelihood the receptionist will have been advised that you are coming and will know who you are there to see.

If you are shown into a waiting room or conference area, temporarily occupy the "lowest" seat, usually the one nearest the door. Do not spread your belongings around as if you were making yourself at home in the meantime. When the person appears, stand and make formal introductions and greetings, then wait until invited to have a seat.

In business and in private life when one needs help in working out some kind of problem or in remedying a mistake there is a greater probability of success if one is humble and "requests" assistance rather than "demanding" that something be done. Whether the problem or mistake was caused by you yourself or by someone else is unimportant. The key question is whether you want something done. If you do, don't rant and rave or loudly insist on your "rights." Calmly ask that something be done to rectify the situation. If you yourself are at fault, the other party will be more willing to assist you if you humbly admit your foolishness. If the other party is at fault, if you give him an opportunity to make amends he will be very grateful. Japan can be a frustrating place at times, but there is no excuse for unloading all of one's frustrations on any single person. Try to treat others as you would like them to treat you when you yourself make a mistake.

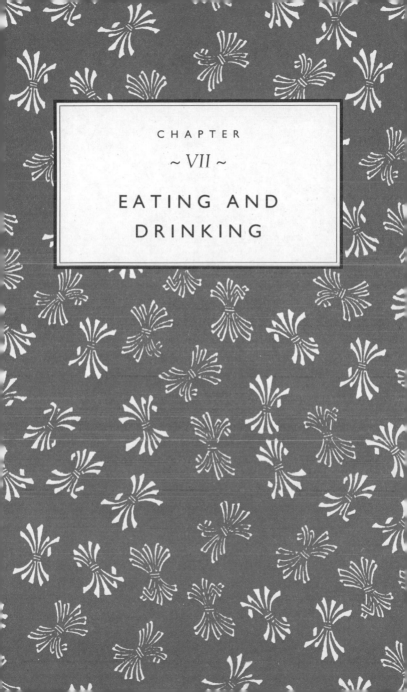

CHAPTER

~ *VII* ~

EATING AND
DRINKING

BEFORE ONE partakes of anything, in virtually any situation, one says *Itadakimasu*, an expression of gratitude for what is presented and to the person who presented it. If one is offered more than a cup of tea, when one has finished one says *Gochisōsama deshita* in appreciation. These two expressions are often accompanied by a slight bow. This holds true for private homes and offices.

If you are eating alone in a restaurant, it is not necessary to verbalize the first expression, but you will use the second expression when you go to the register to pay the bill.

If you are eating with someone, you will wait until everyone is served, then say the first expression. If each person is paying for his own meal (*warikan*), you will use the second expression at the register. If someone else is picking up the tab, you will wait beyond the register or outside the door and say *Gochisōsama* to the person who paid.

~ CHOPSTICKS ~

AS SHOWN in the illustrations, you pick up the chopsticks (*o-hashi*) with one hand, then use both hands to align them. In the third illustration, the left hand is holding the chopsticks, as the right hand is moved

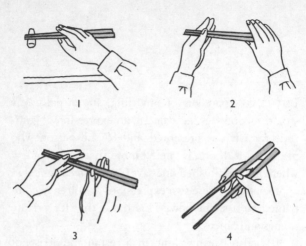

1   2

3   4

back to grip them. The fourth illustration shows the proper placement of the fingers and how far up the chopsticks should be held.

Between bites place chopsticks on the chopstick rest (*hashi-oki*), if there is one, or on the table. One may also place them on the paper sleeve (*hashi-bukuro*) in which they came or on the edge of the tray so that the ends which touch the food do not touch the tray. Generally, Japanese food is served on individual plates for each person, but if you need to take something from a common plate, it is proper to reverse the chopsticks and pick up the item with the opposite ends. In other words, do not use the eating ends when touching something that others will also touch. When you have finished your meal, slip the chopsticks back into the sleeve and fold over one end of the sleeve or place them on the rest.

Chopsticks are not to be left in the mouth after they have delivered the food. They are not to be used for pointing or drawing pictures in the air. They are not to be stuck into food or left sticking into food, especially in rice bowls, as this is done for the deceased at memorial ceremonies. One does not mix food with chopsticks or pick here and there at food.

~ TABLE MANNERS ~

WHEN ONE is offered a cup of green tea, if there is a lid, remove it and place it upside down on the table so that it does not roll. The proper order for serving guests and correct placement of tea, cake, and small dampened towel are shown in the illustrations in the section "Visiting Others at Home," beginning on page 45.

Whether in a restaurant or a home, a casual meal will probably consist of several dishes carefully arranged. It is acceptable to move one dish at a time to make it easier to eat, but do not make a wholesale rearrangement.

Generally commence with the soup and if there is a lid, remove it and place it upside down on the tray or table. If vacuum pressure makes the lid difficult to remove, simply squeeze the top edges of the bowl together. This will release the pressure.

Use the free hand to gently keep plates and trays from sliding and to pick up bowls and saucers when eating from them. One picks up bowls of soup and rice and small plates and dishes with sauce to avoid spilling food. Be careful not to stick your thumb into the bowl

A traditional Japanese meal, consisting of grilled fish, side dish, sashimi, rice, and soup

when picking it up. Particularly when eating food that is dipped in small dishes of sauce, bring the dish close to your mouth and hold it under the food. Do not hold a bowl for a long time between bites. Alternate between dishes, but do not pick here and there rapidly.

When you are eating *nigiri-zushi* (bite-size pieces of sushi), it is acceptable to use your fingers. Often it is easier to eat a piece of sushi made of octopus or fish in one bite. Trying to bite it in two causes more difficulties than stuffing it in your mouth. Also, when you are served a large piece of meat it is often better to pick the piece up and take a bite out of it than to try to cut the piece with chopsticks.

Because tea and soup are often served quite hot, rather than blowing on the food, Japanese make a slurping sound when drinking in order to cool the liquid. Although it is acceptable to slurp, be sure not to exaggerate the noise.

Japanese tend to be less talkative when eating and it is considered improper to talk with food in one's mouth.

The illustration shows the normal placement of Japanese dishes from the view of the person eating. If there is a napkin, it is not for placing on the lap or for wiping the mouth. Rather, it is merely to keep eating utensils from directly touching the table. If there is no napkin, use your handkerchief for wiping your mouth. At the end of the meal, if you must use a toothpick, at least cover your mouth with your free hand.

~ DRINKING ~

IF ALCOHOL is served at a party, the party will officially begin with a toast by the senior member or an honored guest. One raises one's glass or cup and says *kampai*. People sometimes click glasses together. It is perfectly acceptable to join the toast with a glass of juice or soda.

Beer is generally drunk from small glasses and saké is served in small bottles (*tokkuri*) and drunk from small cups (*sakazuki* or *o-choko*). In groups it is customary to pour for others and not for yourself. One shows respect and consideration for others by keeping an eye on the levels of the glasses or cups of those nearby. If you refill a person's cup or glass, he or she will undoubtedly offer to fill yours in return.

The more polite way to serve another is to hold the bottle or *tokkuri* in two hands, one underneath. At more formal gatherings, or as a party moves along, people use one hand for pouring. When one is being poured for, one should always lift one's glass or cup from the table; leaving either on the table when someone is thoughtfully filling it is rude.

With the possible exception of the first glass on a hot day, one should avoid draining a glass of beer at one quaff, as an empty glass may be seen as an indication that you are no longer drinking. If your glass is still partially full and you want to politely indicate that you do not wish to drink more, place your hand over the glass and bow slightly to indicate that you appreciate the other person's kindness anyway. Some people turn the glass or *sakazuki* upside down to indicate that they have had enough.

Although not as common as it used to be, as a gesture of friendship—or because there is no clean glass or *sakazuki*—men will finish off the contents of their own and hand it to the other person and offer to fill it. Should one wish to decline, it is a little awkward, but one can do so with some hastily conceived excuse.

Japanese are unperturbed about alternately drinking saké, beer, and whiskey. It is also considered acceptable for people to "loosen up" under the influence of alcohol. Medical research shows that the vast majority of Japanese lack a certain enzyme whose function is to break down alcohol. As a result of this lack, some people can get quite inebriated in a very short time. It is inappropriate to push others to drink, and one can avoid drinking too much oneself by gratefully sipping a glass whenever it is filled without tossing the whole glass back. Japanese police are extremely strict on drinking and driving, so do not allow anyone to do so.

~ FORMAL BANQUETS ~

AT STAND-UP receptions one is expected to socialize and the filling of another person's glass creates an opportunity to commence a conversation. In large receptions there may be female "companions," ladies whose job it is to fill plates and glasses for guests and make small talk. One does not offer food or drink to them for they are on the job.

Formal, seated Western-style dinners, such as wedding receptions, allow for more restricted socializing, but so long as there is no formal speech being made, it is usually acceptable to rise from your seat and offer drinks to people sitting at other tables. One can tell from the behavior of others whether the situation permits it. When you do leave your seat, place your napkin on the table so others will know the place is taken.

Japanese-style seated banquets require somewhat more formal manners, as one is seated on tatami and eating from raised trays.

At many parties, after the opening speeches and the toast, the gathered may eat and drink for a time, then commence a round of speeches and even songs. Always be prepared to do one or the other.

When a large party comes to a close, the assembled may break into smaller groups to go to "second parties." Sometimes this is to "relax" after the formalities of the larger gathering. If you are invited to go along, you will have an opportunity to get to know a few people in a more relaxed atmosphere and catch up on what is going on behind the scenes.

~ KARAOKE ~

WHETHER DURING a wedding reception or a small gathering of friends, one may be invited to sing to the recorded musical accompaniment of *karaoke*, from *kara* meaning empty and *oke* from the Japanese pronunciation of orchestra. Whether you like to sing or not, do your best when your turn comes, then relinquish the microphone. Whether you have a beautiful voice or are unable to sing three notes in tune, you will have shown your willingness to participate. Do not be misled by great applause; it is not necessary to entertain everyone with several encores.

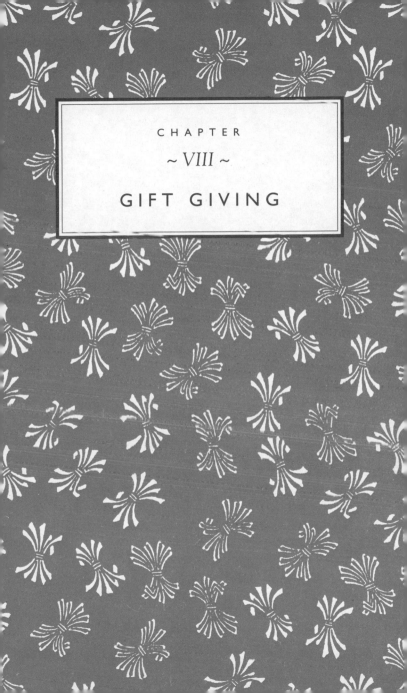

CHAPTER

~ VIII ~

GIFT GIVING

THE EXCHANGE of gifts is a significant part of Japanese social relationships, whether motivated by sincerity, obligation, or something in-between. Sometimes a gift is a way of expressing appreciation for friendship or benefits recently received and sometimes it is more for long-term considerations. Before we go into detail, it is important to point out these guidelines: (1) Virtually every gift one receives calls for a "return gift" (*o-kaeshi*). Most often such a gift is prompt. Minor kindnesses, for example the presentation of a small gift to one's child, may be reciprocated in another form at some later date. (2) The way in which a gift is wrapped and presented is quite important.

First we will discuss occasions for gift giving and the types of appropriate gifts, then the manner of proper presentation. The chart on page 85 shows the details of the wrapping and whether a return gift is appropriate. For details of gift giving at weddings and funerals, see pages 98 and 109 respectively.

~ O-CHŪGEN AND ~
O-SEIBO

BEFORE DESCRIBING the more specific occasions of gift giving, we want to call attention to the nationally observed gift "seasons" during which virtually everyone gives and receives presents. There are two major gift-giving seasons, the first being *o-chūgen*, which extends from the latter weeks of June through early July. This is a time for thanking people for their patronage and help. Businesses have department stores send these gifts of appreciation to regular clients, and families use this opportunity to thank relatives, certain friends to whom they are obligated, piano teachers, etc.

O-seibo, the second major gift-giving season of the year, continues from about the end of November through the third week of December. Department stores tend to be very busy on the first weekend of December because employees receive winter bonuses and people order gifts at that time, so be forewarned.

Popular gifts for *o-chūgen* and *o-seibo* vary from year to year, but the price range from three thousand to five thousand yen seems stable. How much one should spend for a gift depends on the nature of the relationship, the age of the giver, and the economic situation of the giver. Those on the younger side of forty keep toward the lower end of the range. Those who are older and better able to afford it tend to be more generous. A gift of three thousand yen is appropriate for most people and five thousand yen for special patrons or benefactors. It is not a case of more is better. Overdoing in gift giving simply makes the other person feel it is necessary to somehow balance the books with a return gift.

Regardless of the amount spent, appropriate packaging makes the gift look better. From this point of view, a bottle of whiskey wrapped in paper from a major department store is more impressive than the same whiskey from the local liquor store. Although people used to present such gifts in person, it is now common to make use of the convenient home-delivery services (*takuhaibin*). Especially if a gift is heavy, it is considerate to have it delivered to the home of the recipient.

Special seasonal gifts for summer include juice and fruit and for winter include salmon and pickles (*tsuke-mono*). Perennial favorites through both seasons include green or black tea, seaweed (*nori*), coffee, jam, meats and hams, fish, crab, cheese and butter, juice, canned fruit, salad oil, soy sauce, wine, whiskey, brandy, beer, saké, cookies, candy, bath soap, towels, plates, and gift certificates and coupons for such things as books, beer, and dairy products. Almost all of the items above are sold in special sets that go on display in June or November for delivery during the gift-giving season. The stores will arrange to have the proper wrapping placed on each and will have the packages delivered, so take your address book.

~ OTHER GIFT ~ OCCASIONS

ONE USUALLY gives gifts in celebration of the birth of a child, the attainment of the ages of seven, five, and three (*shichi-go-san*), success in entering schools (nyūgaku), marriage, and the celebration of the New Year.

You may congratulate parents on the birth of a child by sending a gift between seven days after birth and the end of the first month after birth. Typical presents include specially packaged sets of clothing for children, priced around five thousand yen. Parents may respond with an *uchi-iwai* gift of *sekihan* (rice specially cooked with red beans). Often such gifts are eventually "repaid" by gifts to one's own children or in other ways.

At *shichi-go-san*, families in which daughters attain the ages of three and seven and sons attain the age of five celebrate the event on or around November 15 by dressing up, visiting a local shrine, and taking pictures. This is a family affair, but close family friends sometimes offer congratulations by giving small presents of money, clothing, or toys. Parents respond with an *uchi-iwai* gift of *chitose-ame* (a special stick candy) or *sekihan*. Return gifts on occasions like *shichi-go-san* should include as the sender the first name of the child who was feted.

When children enter kindergarten, elementary school, middle school, high school, and university, relatives and friends may congratulate the child with a gift of money, stationery, or book coupons (*toshoken*). Graduation gifts include accessories, gift certificates, and money.

Before we leave the children behind, we should note that parents, friends, and relatives often give gifts of money (*o-toshidama*) to children in special envelopes on the occasion of the New Year. If one visits a family at this time, it is proper to prepare some small o-toshidama for each child up through high school, *if* you are a close friend of the family. No special return gift is necessary, but usually the favor is returned in one way or another.

When one is invited to a wedding reception it is proper to take a gift of money in a special envelope to the reception. It is not customary to bring a present in addition to or instead of money. If you do wish to give a gift in addition to money, have it sent to the family several days prior to the wedding or within the first year of marriage. Each person who attends the reception will be given a return gift called *hikide-mono* in a bag to make it easy to carry. In general, if one is invited to a reception but is unable to attend, one sends a gift later. Specifics of wedding gifts can be found in the chapter on weddings, beginning on page 93.

Gifts in celebration of a promotion include accessories, wine, whiskey, and sporting goods.

If you are taking a trip abroad or in Japan, you might want to bring back local products or specialty products to family members, friends, or colleagues. These souvenirs (*o-miyage*) can serve as expressions of appreciation for some earlier favor and are not so formal as other gifts, so price is not as important.

When you visit a home, it is proper to take along fruit, cake, cookies, candy, or other kinds of food.

~ MISFORTUNES ~

WHEN SOMEONE passes away, one usually takes a gift of money to either the wake or to the funeral itself. If one can attend neither, it is acceptable to mail it in a special envelope which is placed in the postal service's envelope for registered mail (*genkin kakitome*). Specifics can be found in the section "Condolence Gifts," beginning on page 109.

When someone has suffered damage from a natural disaster or a fire, one should go immediately and offer assistance in the appropriate clothes for actually helping. Taking along canned or easily prepared food and offering a place to stay are both ways to be kind. Since disasters are times when people can use cash, a gift of money will also be appreciated. No return gifts are necessary.

If someone has become ill, one can take an envelope of money, half of which will generally be returned in some form upon recovery from the illness.

~ GIFT ENVELOPES AND ~ WRAPPINGS

A NON-JAPANESE should not become anxious about doing everything letter-perfect as far as the etiquette of gift giving is concerned, but we include in this section and in the illustrations information about the proper way to do everything related to the "packaging" of both money and actual gifts.

A personal gift to a friend on a birthday may be wrapped in ordinary Western-style wrapping paper and tied with a ribbon, but for more formal occasions there are traditional ways of wrapping presents.

First a gift is wrapped in ordinary wrapping paper, then covered with a sheet of white paper. Around this are tied the formal decorative stiff paper strings called *mizuhiki*. Often the design of this decoration is printed on the white paper, but this is more informal. The paper cords for ordinary felicitous occasions are red and white and those for weddings are gold and silver or gold and red. The cords for funerals are black and white.

The *mizuhiki* on envelopes you buy are already tied. Bows for felicitous occasions are tied in the *chō-musubi* style, which looks somewhat like a butterfly's wings. The elaborate method of tying indicates one's desire that the felicity long continue. Bows for infelicitous events are tied in the simple *musubikiri* style (page 86), with the ends cut, indicating the hope that the event not occur again.

As shown in the illustration on the following page, there is an appropriate inscription (*omotegaki*) above the knot of the *mizuhiki*. To the right of this inscription on more formal gifts is a decoration called *noshi*. This is a narrow strip of dried abalone wrapped in red and white paper or a printed image thereof. Below the knot is written the name of the giver(s).

Gifts of money are given in cash and not in check form. They are inserted in special envelopes called *noshi-bukuro* or *shūgi-bukuro*. An assortment of inexpensive envelopes may be found at convenience stores, but the more expensive and more elaborate ones are sold in department stores and stationery stores. The elaborateness of the envelope should be matched by the contents. A fancy envelope with slim

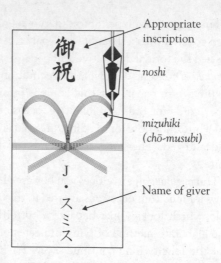

Appropriate inscription

noshi

mizuhiki (*chō-musubi*)

Name of giver

contents is not appropriate, so you should choose an envelope style that is appropriate for the amount of money you are giving. In general, the larger the amount, the more elaborate the envelope.

A common concern is exactly how much to give to whom. As always, this depends on your economic status, your age and position, and the age and position of the other person. In the respective sections on weddings and funerals we include tables with suggestions of the ranges.

Please refer to the accompanying chart for guidance about proper wording for gifts and envelopes, types of *mizuhiki*, and whether or not *noshi* should be attached. Also indicated are those occasions when return gifts are appropriate.

FESTIVITY	WORDING	PRESENT	MIZUHIKI
New Year's *o-chūgen* *o-seibo*	御年賀 御中元 御歳暮	 (gift)	red & white *chō-musubi*
birth	御祝い 御出産祝	 (gift) (money)	red & white *chō-musubi*
(return gift)	内祝	 (gift)	red & white *chō-musubi*
shichi-go-san school entrance graduation	御祝い 御入学祝 御卒業祝	 (money)	red & white *chō-musubi*
DIFFICULTY	WORDING	PRESENT	MIZUHIKI
natural disaster fire	御見舞 御伺い	 (money)	(none)
illness	御見舞	 (money)	(none)
(return gift)	快気祝		red & white *musubikiri*

85

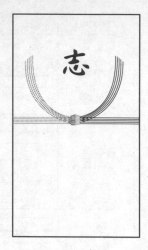

This type of envelope is given by the family of the deceased to the priest, driver, or other person who assisted at a funeral. The bow with the ends cut off is tied in the musubikiri style, indicating the giver's hope that the unhappy event not be repeated.

This paper with the bow in the musubikiri style is placed around a return gift by a person who had earlier been given something when he or she was sick.

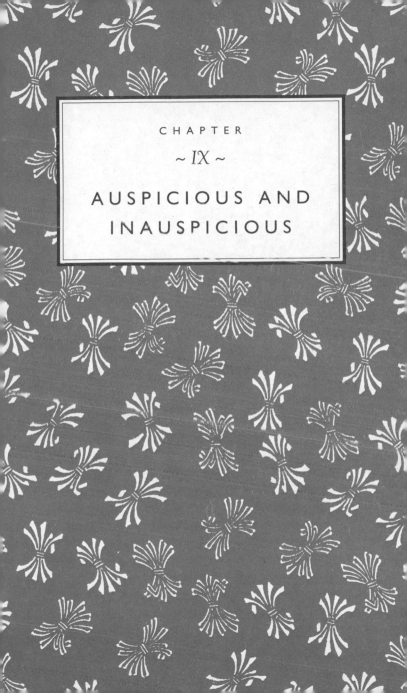

CHAPTER

~ IX ~

AUSPICIOUS AND
INAUSPICIOUS

~ NUMBERS ~

THE NUMBERS one, three, five, and seven are considered
auspicious numbers and the number two seems generally neutral to Japanese. In contrast, the numbers four
(*shi*) and nine (*ku*) are considered inauspicious because they echo the words for death and hardship,
respectively. Buddhist services for a deceased family
member, for example, are held on the forty-ninth day
after death.

When one gives a gift of money, it is almost always
in the amount of one of the auspicious numbers. When
one takes flowers to someone in the hospital, it is best
to avoid flowers in inauspicious numbers. While we
are on the subject of flowers, there is also a disinclina-
tion to give a hospital patient white flowers, flowers
whose blossoms may suddenly drop off, like camellias,
and potted plants, which might encourage the patient
to "take root" in the bed.

Yaku-doshi are those ages which are traditionally
regarded as unlucky or somehow critical for adults.
The most widely recognized of these are twenty-five
and forty-two for men and nineteen and thirty-three
for women. To protect themselves from bad luck or
disaster some people of these ages worship at shrines or
temples and in general try to avoid taking unnecessary
risks.

The good years are celebrated during the seven-
five-three (*shichi-go-san*) festival for children and later

89

in life at sixty *(kanreki)*, seventy *(koki)*, seventy-seven *(kiju)*, eighty-eight *(beiju)*, and ninety-nine *(hakuju)*.

There are complex rules determining the number of strokes required to write names, a factor many parents consider when they decide the characters of the names they give their children.

Though there is no special connotation involved we would note that eggs come in tens and in Japan there is no particular attraction to lumping things in lots of a dozen. Also, although English tends to divide numbers in hundreds, thousands, and millions—as indicated by commas—Japanese counting is heavily dependent on ten thousands *(man)* and ten millions *(oku)*.

~ COLORS ~

THE STANDARD dress for men at both weddings and funerals is a black suit and white shirt. At weddings men wear white ties, and at funerals they wear black ties. Women wedding guests may wear a black background kimono with a gold, silver, or multicolored pattern, and a plain black silk kimono without a design to a funeral.

Colors are important when it comes to the envelopes that one places gifts of money in. The twisted paper strings *(mizuhiki)* that are wrapped around the envelope or represented in printed form on the envelope are red and white for ordinary felicitous occasions, gold and silver or gold and red for marriage ceremonies, and black and white for funerals.

~ CALENDAR DAYS ~

CALENDARS PRINTED in Japan may show the *rokki*, the six-day cycle of auspicious and inauspicious days for the main events of life. Although Japanese may not think of themselves as being religious or superstitious, they will choose to become engaged, wed, start new businesses, and start construction of houses on auspicious days. The cycle is *senkachi*, *tomobiki*, *senmake*, *butsumetsu*, *taian*, and *shakkō*.

Senkachi, or *senshō*, literally means early victory and is considered an auspicious day for urgent business and lawsuits, but the afternoon is inauspicious. *Tomobiki* is generally auspicious, except for midday, but is inauspicious for funerals because of the idea that one might "pull a friend" (*tomodachi o hiku*) along into death. *Senmake*, or *senbu*, literally means early defeat, so one should avoid doing urgent business and filing lawsuits in the morning, but the afternoon hours are auspicious. *Butsumetsu* is a completely inauspicious day, so no one opens a new shop, changes houses, or starts new enterprises on this day. *Taian*, or *daian*, literally means great peace and is a perfect day for doing anything, so wedding chapels are extremely busy on this day. *Shakkō*, or *shakku*, is an auspicious day, except for midday. Though a young couple may care little for the auspiciousness of particular days, the chances are that with so many people being involved in their wedding and the reception, they will end up selecting an auspicious day for the ceremonies.

12		
199X		
水	**1**	先勝
木	**2**	友引
金	**3**	先負
土	**4**	仏滅
日	**5**	大安
月	**6**	赤口

The calendar shows the six-day cycle of auspicious and inauspicious days, beginning with senkachi, *followed by* tomobiki, senmake, butsumetsu, taian, *and* shakkō.

7-5-3	七五三	shichi-go-san
61	還暦	kanreki
70	古稀	koki
77	喜寿	kiju
88	米寿	beiju
99	白寿	hakuju

The chart lists years of one's life considered auspicious by most Japanese.

CHAPTER

~ X ~

WEDDINGS

THE TRADITIONS of marriage in Japan involve the activities of a go-between (*baishakunin* or *nakōdo*) at some point. In the case of an arranged marriage (*miai kekkon*), the go-between may actually introduce the two young people for the first time. If two people on their own decide to get married (*ren'ai kekkon*), they will eventually ask someone to act as a go-between at the wedding ceremony and the following reception. Depending upon how early on the go-between becomes involved, the couple is more or less indebted to the person and the go-between's responsibilities are heavier or lighter.

Formal engagement ceremonies (*yuinō*) are held to exchange betrothal gifts between the families of the prospective bride and groom. The gifts, formally wrapped and presented, may include traditionally auspicious items such as sea bream or casks of saké or betrothal gift money. It should be pointed out that marriage in Japan is, to a larger degree than in some other countries, a relation involving families. The go-between is very often called upon to work out differences of opinion in how to hold the ceremonies and who should do what.

Japanese weddings consist of short ceremonies (*kekkon shiki*) attended by a few relatives and friends followed by a large reception (*kekkon hirōen*) and a sit-down dinner attended by large numbers of people related to the two families. Unless specifically invited to the ceremony itself, guests are usually invited to just the reception. This should not be taken as an indication of how the couple sees their relationship to the other guests. It is simply that the ceremonial halls are often quite small.

96

A formal invitation may or may not be preceded by a verbal announcement of the event and an invitation to attend. If you are married, to avoid potential embarrassment, ascertain whether you alone or you and your spouse are being invited. The person(s) to whom the written invitation is addressed will make this clear.

Front of postcard

When the formal invitation comes, it will most likely include a pre-addressed R.S.V.P. post-

Accepting   *Declining*

card. Printed on the invitation is the date by which the couple would like to receive your response, so even if you have given a verbal reply, mail the card before the date requested. The families have to make final arrangements with the reception hall, print a list of the names of those attending, and prepare gifts for those guests. On the front of the postcard you cross out the character *yuki* (to) and write in the character for the honorific *-sama*. On the back of the postcard you cross out the character for either accept or decline and also cross out the honorifics referring to yourself, as shown in the illustration. If you plan to attend, add a note of congratulations along with your address and name. If you cannot attend, add a note of regret.

Should you be unable to attend the reception, you may wish to follow custom and send a congratulatory telegram (*o-iwai dempō*). Dial 115 and order a telegram to be sent so that it arrives at the wedding hall or the family home well prior to the wedding itself. You can order as early as ten days ahead of the day of delivery. Set messages may be found in the back of the NTT directory, each with a number to make ordering very simple. Examples include:

001: *Gokekkon omedetō gozaimasu.* (Congratulations on your wedding.)

015: Congratulations on your happy wedding.

In general, one also sends a congratulatory gift to the new couple even if one cannot attend the reception. This may be sent to the couple's home anytime within the first months of marriage. If you do attend the reception, you should take a gift of money in a special envelope (*shūgi-bukuro*) with the inscription

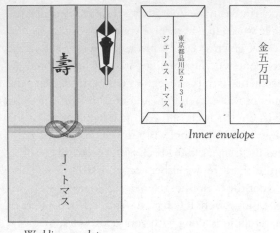

壽

J・トマス

Wedding envelope

東京都品川区2−3−4
ジェームス・トマス

Inner envelope

金五万円

for felicitations (*kotobuki*), as shown in the illustration. As for the contents, the chart gives some idea of the range that is generally recognized. If you are younger, you may take the lower figure as an indication of what is proper. An older person with social status may take the higher figure as appropriate. New bills,

RELATION TO YOU	ATTENDING RECEPTION	NOT ATTENDING
Immediate family	¥30,000–70,000	¥10,000–50,000
Relative	¥30,000–70,000	¥10,000–50,000
Friend	¥10,000–30,000	¥10,000
Colleague	¥20,000–30,000	¥5,000–10,000
Subordinate	¥10,000–20,000	¥10,000–20,000
Client	¥20,000–30,000	¥20,000–30,000
Benefactor	¥10,000–20,000	¥5,000–10,000

Monetary wedding gifts

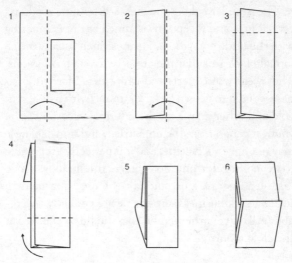

Folding the outer envelope

still unfolded, should be placed in an inner envelope that is folded as in the illustrations above. If the envelope which you purchase for the occasion at a stationery store or department store has an inner envelope, simply slip the bills in that. It is important to write the amount of the money and your name and address so that there is no confusion with so many people attending and presenting gifts. The illustrations on the opposite page show the proper place for writing your name and address and the amount written in Chinese characters. In the process of removing the inner envelope, you may have forgotten how the outer envelope was folded. As shown in the above illustrations, it is important that the bottom flap be folded upward on top of the upper flap.

The standard dress for guests attending wedding ceremonies and receptions is aimed at not competing with the bride and groom. Japanese men usually own a formal black suit that they reserve for such occasions. They wear white shirts and white ties. Married Japanese women may own a black kimono with a design in gold and other colors for these formal occasions. The younger generation, the unmarried, and non-Japanese may not have such attire, and it is perfectly acceptable to wear other clothing. For women, this includes a nice knee-length dress or suit and blouse. For men, a regular, dark business suit and tie are perfectly acceptable. All outer garments and bags should be checked at the cloakroom.

~ THE WEDDING ~
CEREMONY

THERE ARE three types of wedding ceremonies: Shinto, Christian, and Buddhist. Shinto ceremonies involve the active participation of only the priest, bride, groom, close relatives, and go-between couple, so if you are invited to attend, you need only watch and follow the example of other guests. Christian weddings involve more participation in the form of standing and singing, but little else. Buddhist ceremonies are rare.

The wedding ceremony itself may be held in a shrine, church, or temple, or in a hotel or "wedding hall," where the event can be held just prior to the reception.

~ THE WEDDING ~
RECEPTION

WEDDING RECEPTIONS are carefully orchestrated affairs and one should be sure to arrive in advance of the appointed time. Near the entrance to the banquet hall will be a reception table.

The people sitting at the reception table are most likely to be young friends of the bride and groom. Turn the envelope with your money gift so that it faces the reception attendant and place it on the tray provided, sign the guest book, and accept a copy of the printed program of the reception. As a reminder, it is not customary to bring a present in addition to money because there is no provision for handling such things at the reception. The printed program you receive will have the order of the reception events and a seating arrangement showing the names of every person in attendance along with some indication of how they are related to the couple or their families. Note where you are to be seated and who else will sit at the same table.

Generally an announcement will be made that the preparations are complete and that everyone should sit down. A formal introduction of the bride and groom and announcement of their wedding will be given by the go-between, and a toast will follow. Then come two or three hours of speeches, songs, eating, drinking, and congratulations. If you have been requested to give a speech, you should make it brief and polite. When called on by the master of ceremonies, you should rise, bow simply to the others at your table, and walk to the indicated microphone. Bow to the assembled, keep your congratulations sincere and short, bow to the couple and the assembled, and return to your seat.

Whether or not you give a congratulatory message, you may wish to offer more personal congratulations to the bride and groom. During a lull in the speeches and songs, take a bottle of beer or saké from your table and go to the head table. Fill the newlyweds' glasses as an excuse for saying *O-medetō gozaimasu*. During the reception the bride will probably leave the banquet several times to change her attire (*o-ironaoshi*), so if you want to congratulate both bride and groom, don't wait too long.

Usually the parents of the bride and groom will make the rounds of the tables filling glasses of the guests. You should offer them polite congratulations as well.

As the party draws to a conclusion, a server may come to your table and package some of the untouched food and place it in the bag near your chair which contains the "return gift" (in this case called *hikide-mono*) that you will carry home. At the conclusion of the dinner, take your bag and head to the exit where the bride and groom and their parents will bid you a formal farewell and thank you for attending. Bow, offer a final *O-medetō gozaimasu*, and depart.

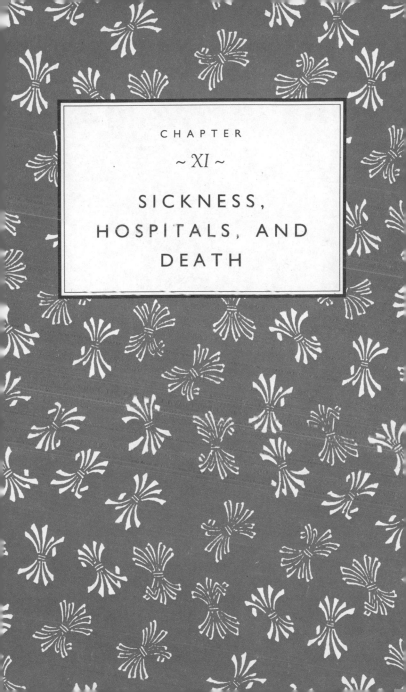

CHAPTER

~ XI ~

SICKNESS, HOSPITALS, AND DEATH

~ VISITING A HOSPITAL ~

BEFORE VISITING someone in the hospital, one should find out whether the person is well enough to receive visitors and whether the person wants visitors. Some people would rather not have others see them while they are ill. Furthermore, one should not make a visit just prior to or immediately after someone has had surgery. If the person is willing and able to accept visitors, one should visit only during visiting hours set by the hospital for that particular ward.

Whether the patient is in a private room or a ward, as is more likely in Japan, one should be considerate toward other patients as well as the person you are calling on. If you wish to take something as a get-well gift on your visit (*o-mimai*), avoid potted plants (which inauspiciously suggest a long stay for the patient), avoid flowers in fours and nines, avoid flowers whose blossoms might suddenly drop off, like camellias, avoid flowers altogether for patients with allergies, avoid expensive items that might prove tempting to a thief, and confirm restrictions on diet before selecting a food item. Avoid taking young children along unless absolutely necessary as they may make noise and otherwise disturb other patients.

In a shared room, when you enter be sure to greet every patient with a bow and *O-jama shimasu*. It may have taken you a long time to reach the hospital, so you may be tempted to stay a while, but remember that no matter how well meant a long visit may be it is a strain on the patient and others in the room. Patients are in the hospital to rest and recuperate, so make your visit brief. If the patient is to be hospitalized for a long time, you can show your concern by returning several times.

106

As you leave, you may say *O-daiji ni* to the person you have visited and *O-jama shimashita* to the other patients.

~ STAYING ~

IF YOU yourself need to be hospitalized, the attending nurse will give you specific information concerning what to bring with you. As a general rule you should prepare the following for your stay: pajamas, slippers, and dressing robe (for moving about the hospital), toothbrush and toothpaste, a wash bowl and soap, face towel and bath towel, essential changes of clothing, a small amount of money for incidentals, and your insurance card (*hokenshō*) if you have one. You do not want to have unnecessary items because there is little storage space.

~ DEATH ~

WHEN SOMEONE passes away, a physician issues a certificate of death (*shibō shindanshō*) to which is attached a death notification (*shibō todoke*), which should be filled out and submitted to the local ward or city office within seven days. When this is submitted, one also applies for a permit (*shitai kasō kyokashō*) to dispose of the deceased's body, usually by cremation. The family contacts a funeral director (*sōgiya* or *sōgisha*), who will make all of the arrangements for the wake, funeral, and cremation.

107

The family notifies those people they feel should be directly contacted and perhaps asks these people to notify others. Announcements of formal ceremonies for well-known figures may appear in the newspaper, but normally communication is done by word of mouth. The family may not know all of the deceased's acquaintances and colleagues, so those who hear the news should notify others they feel should be informed.

When one receives notification of a death, one should respond as quickly as possible, and at all times consider the feelings of the bereaved. The general pattern for final rites is the viewing of the body, the wake (*tsuya*), the funeral (*sōgi*), and the cremation, followed by interment and several ceremonies of remembrance over the following months and years. Which of these events one participates in depends on the degree of one's involvement with the deceased and the bereaved family. An acquaintance might attend either the wake or the funeral service. A close friend or relative might help out in the home throughout the wake and attend the other ceremonies as well. Generally only family members attend the memorial services. The family will ask one person to be in charge of the proceedings and help everyone do the appropriate thing at the appropriate time.

If one is unable to attend the wake or the funeral, it is polite to send a telegram of condolence (*o-kuyami dempō*). Telegrams can be billed to a private phone by dialing 115 between the hours of 8:00 a.m. and 10:00 p.m. Normal delivery hours are between 8:00 a.m. and 7:00 p.m. Telegrams ordered before 7:00 p.m. will be delivered that day and those ordered after 7:00 p.m. will be delivered the following day. In the back of the NTT directory are sample telegrams which can be ordered by number. Two samples and the numbers for ordering them follow:

> 500: *Tsutsushinde aitō no i o hyō shimasu.* (I express my deepest sympathy.)
>
> 501: *Goseikyo o itami, tsutsushinde o-kuyami mōshi-agemasu.* (I offer my deepest sympathy at this time of bereavement.)

~ CLOTHING ~

AS WAKES are often rather sudden occasions the manners concerning dress are less rigid than for formal funerals for which attendees have sufficient time to prepare. Where possible men wear a black suit to wakes and funerals and where not possible it is acceptable to wear dark brown, dark blue, or dark gray with a black or dark tie. Women wear a black or dark one-piece dress, suit and blouse, or skirt and blouse. When you attend a wake directly from the workplace, for example, it is acceptable to go as one is dressed, but men make an effort to at least change to a subdued necktie and women remove extra makeup and jewelry.

Since there is more time to prepare for a funeral, one should be as formally attired as possible. Women wear formal black kimono or a black or dark one-piece dress, suit and blouse, or skirt and blouse. Women should avoid much makeup, jewelry, perfume, and bright colors. Men wear black or dark gray, dark brown, or dark blue suits and black or dark ties. To be especially proper some wear formal mourning attire.

When one attends a wake or funeral, one should make every effort to have briefcases, parcels, or luggage checked at a train station or left at a friend's house before proceeding to the service.

~ CONDOLENCE GIFTS ~

THE CONDOLENCE gift (*kōden*) is offered as money for incense and may be taken either to the wake or the funeral. To be proper, one should place the money in a special envelope (*kōden-bukuro* or *bushūgi-bukuro*), as shown in the illustration, and carried to the ceremony

Condolence-money envelopes: Buddhist, Christian, Shinto

東京都杉並区
荻窪2－3－4
田中直子

金五万円

Reverse of envelope

in a special carrying cloth called a *fukusa*. Appropriate envelopes with black and white or silver and white twisted paper strings (*mizuhiki*), which are left untied at the ends, are available at department stores and stationery shops. Because wakes are sudden events, one may have to settle for a less formal envelope available at convenience stores. The cloth is not absolutely necessary, but if you do not use one, take care not to allow the envelope to become soiled or wrinkled. Remove it

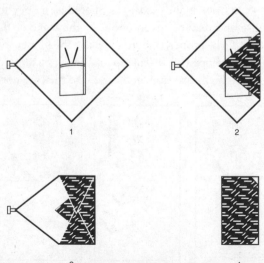

Folding a fukusa

from your pocket or handbag before approaching the reception table or the altar, depending on where it is to be presented.

The table below gives relevant information concerning the contents of the envelope, and the illustrations on page 109 show how it should be prepared for the respective religions. The amount one gives depends on one's status, one's relationship to the deceased and the family, and one's age. Younger people might choose a lower figure, while older people and those with higher social standing might choose a higher figure within the range suggested.

RELATION TO YOU	AMOUNT
Parent	¥50,000–70,000
Brother or sister	¥30,000–50,000
Grandparent	¥10,000–20,000
Relative	¥5,000–10,000
Friend	¥5,000–10,000
Neighbor	¥3,000–5,000
Colleague	¥5,000–10,000

~ WHAT TO SAY ~

AT THE reception table of the wake or the funeral, one can make a simple greeting of condolence to those who are helping out by saying *Kono tabi wa tonda koto de* or *O-mairi sasete itadakimasu* (basically, you are sorry to hear about the death, or you have come to pay your respects).

To the family of the bereaved, upon seeing them on the first occasion after the death, one might say *Kono tabi wa omoimokakenai koto de, kokoro kara o-kuyami mōshiagemasu* or *O-torikomi chū to zonjimasu ga, hitokoto o-kuyami o mōshiagetaku, o-ukagai shimashita* (basically, you would like to express your condolences for such a sudden misfortune).

At the wake one might say *Kokoro kara o-kuyami mōshiagemasu. O-yaku ni tateru koto ga arimashitara, nannari to omōshitsuke kudasai* (basically, you would like to express your condolences and would be very happy to help in any way possible).

Expressions that are especially taboo throughout these greetings include words that mean repetition or reoccurrence such as *kasanegasane, futatabi,* and *tabitabi.*

~ HELPING OUT ~

ALTHOUGH THE funeral director will handle most of the arrangements for the wake, funeral, and cremation, there is still a lot to be done around the home during the days following death. If one is a particularly close friend of the family or a subordinate of the deceased at the workplace, one generally offers to help out whenever possible. Women usually help out in the kitchen and men assist with the preparations for the wake and setting up of the reception table. If one can help in receiving flowers from delivery services, cooking food for the assembled, cleaning in preparation for the wake, and answering the telephone, it will be appreciated. If you cannot be helpful in such ways, refrain from offering assistance.

~ VIEWING THE BODY ~

THE BODY is placed in one room in a futon with a white cloth covering the face. *If one is invited to view the body, one follows these steps*: (1) Sit formally on the tatami and bow to the family of the deceased. (2) When a member of the family raises the cloth, lean forward to look at the face of the deceased. Never raise the white cloth yourself. (3) Make a deep bow to the body. (4) Slide back slightly, bow toward the family, and leave the room.

It is acceptable to decline an invitation to view the body by saying *Amarinimo tsurai no de* (basically, you find it too sad to do so).

~ THE WAKE ~

THE WAKE is an opportunity for family, friends, and colleagues to gather and mourn the dead. Wakes generally start between 6:00 and 7:00 p.m. and are usually held in the home of the deceased. Those planning to attend should arrive before the service starts and take their leave before 10:00 p.m. even if they are invited to stay for the light supper that is usually provided. Saké and other forms of alcohol may be served, but one should imbibe in moderate amounts.

There will generally be a reception table with a condolence book near the entrance of the house. After making a brief greeting to the person at the reception desk, sign the condolence book or present a name card with the lower left corner folded back. If there is no reception, make your expressions of condolence to the family or the person who has been asked to serve as head mourner, and ask where you might offer your condolence gift.

The proceedings of the wake vary according to the religious practices of the family. The wakes we describe are the standard patterns of the Buddhist and Christian types.

In a Buddhist wake, the family members and close friends sit closest to the altar and others sit in order of their arrival. In some wakes a censer is passed around and each person places some incense in the burner and passes it on. Whether or not this is also done, there is an individual offering of incense at the altar. When it comes time for this, follow these steps: (1) Place your hands together in prayer. (2) Pick up one stick of incense in your right hand and light it from the candle. Unless there are numerous people at the gathering, it is permissible to light two or three stick of incense. (3) Wave out the flame of the incense with the other hand. (4) Place the incense sticks in the ashes of the incense holder one at a time. (5) Bow with your hands together.

In the Christian ceremony, the minister or priest

Offering incense at a Buddhist wake

begins with the reading of scripture and the offering of
a message. The assembled may join in hymns. Instead
of presenting incense, those gathered present a white
chrysanthemum or carnation, following these steps:
(1) Take the carnation and bow to the altar. Turn the
carnation so that the blossom is pointed toward you
and the stem is toward the altar. (2) Place the flower
on the altar. (3) Bow in silent prayer, back away, bow
to the family and the priest or minister, and return to
your seat. (See similar procedure on page 119.)

~ FUNERALS ~

REGARDLESS OF the type of funeral, one should make sure to arrive before the start of the service. Make a brief expression of condolence at the reception table and present your condolence gift, if you have not done so earlier at the wake. It is not appropriate to search out members of the family of the deceased to express your condolences at this juncture as they will likely be preoccupied.

In the Buddhist manner, the funeral service (*sōgi*) consists of the entrance of the priest or priests, opening words, reading of the scriptures, speeches of condolence, reading of telegrams of condolence, offering of incense, and closing words.

A subsequent farewell service called the *kokubetsu-shiki* consists of the mourners offering incense, the departure of the priests, and the closing declaration. The assembled offer incense one by one, as shown in the illustrations: (1) Bow to the priest and the bereaved. (2) In the tatami room, kneel before reaching the altar completely and bow deeply, then proceed closer to the altar. (3) With the thumb and forefinger take a pinch of powdered incense, raise it to eye level, then lower your hand and drop the incense on the incense burner. How many pinches of incense one offers depends on the sect of Buddhism, but generally two or three times is the rule. (4) Place your hands together in prayer, slide backward from the altar, bow again to the priest and family, and return to your seat.

Attending a Buddhist funeral

The Shinto-style funeral consists of purifying one-self with water (*temizu no gi*), purification by the priest (*ōharai no gi*), offering of drink and food to the gods, ceremony by the priest, singing of hymns, and offering of twigs of an auspicious plant.

You purify your hands with water by taking the dipper in the right hand and pouring water three times on the left hand. Then take the dipper in the left hand and pour water on the right hand. Returning the dipper to the right hand, you place some water in the palm of the left hand and rinse your mouth. Rinse the left hand one more time and wipe your mouth with special paper called *kaishi*.

You offer the twigs of the auspicious plant as shown in the illustrations: (1) Hold the twig in two hands, one supporting the leaves. (2) Go to the altar and bow. (3) Turn the twig clockwise and place it on the altar with the leaf end toward you. (4) Take three steps backward, bow twice, place your hands together twice without making a sound, and bow once more.

1 2

3 4

Offering twigs at a Shinto funeral

Offering flowers at a Christian funeral

The Catholic *sōgi* consists of the moving of the casket from the home to the church, the mass, and hymns. The continuing *kokubetsu-shiki* consists of speeches of condolence, the reading of telegrams, speeches by the family, and the offering of flowers.

The Protestant *sōgi* ceremony consists of the entrance of the casket and the family, hymn, scripture reading, prayer, hymn, summary of the deceased's life, sermon, prayer, speeches and reading of telegrams, hymn, prayer, postlude, and greetings by the family. The *kokubetsu-shiki* is the same as the Catholic ceremony described previously.

One offers flowers as in the illustrations: (1, 2) Turn the flower so that the blossom is toward you, place it on the altar, and offer a silent prayer. (3) Step backward, bow to the priest or minister, and return to your seat.

~ SPEECHES ~

IF YOU are asked to give a funeral address, accept graciously. Usually such speeches are written and read aloud, but one may also deliver the message extemporaneously. Mention your relationship to the deceased and speak as a representative of the assembled by straightforwardly expressing the grief of the assembled. Speak clearly and try not to be carried away by emotion. Avoid overstatement, mention of the cause of death, or reference to any failure on the part of the deceased. Also, take into consideration the religious sensibilities of the deceased, the bereaved, and the others who are assembled.

~ REMOVAL OF THE ~ CASKET

IT IS PARTICULARLY respectful to wait outside the funeral site to send off the casket. It is polite to remain quiet and avoid discussion of other affairs while you are waiting. When the casket passes by, bow politely. Unless it is extremely cold, it is polite to refrain from wearing overcoats.

~ AT THE CREMATORY ~

THOSE WHO accompany the casket to the crematory follow the directions of the person in charge. Once the body is inside the furnace, the assembled place items belonging to the deceased on the small table in front of the furnace and light incense.

When the cremation is complete, the assembled will in pairs use bamboo chopsticks to transfer the remains to an urn. The closest remaining relative will at the end place the Adam's apple in the urn, so refrain from touching that.

Following the farewell ceremony, mourners may be offered a white handkerchief and a packet of salt. The salt is to be used for purifying oneself, and the way in which this is done varies. Some simply wash their hands and sprinkle the salt over themselves before going into their homes, while others also gargle. Should salt not be provided, mourners may have it prepared at home.

After these various events, it is advisable to go straight home and change clothes before going to other activities. The reason for this is to avoid mixing the unfelicitous with everyday life.

When the funeral is over, the family of the deceased gives either a monetary or actual gift to the people who assisted and to the people in charge of the ceremonies.

~ MEMORIAL SERVICES ~

MEMORIAL SERVICES and ceremonies are primarily for the families of the departed and are usually small, private affairs.

Buddhists observe memorial services (*hōji*) on the seventh, thirty-fifth, and forty-ninth days after the funeral and on the first, third, seventh, thirteenth, and thirty-third anniversaries.

Shinto observances are held on the tenth day, hundredth day, and the first, third, and fifth anniversaries of the death.

Catholic ceremonies are held on the third day, seventh day, thirtieth day, and the first anniversary of the day of death. Protestant services can occur during the first week or on the tenth day after the death, then one month after the death.

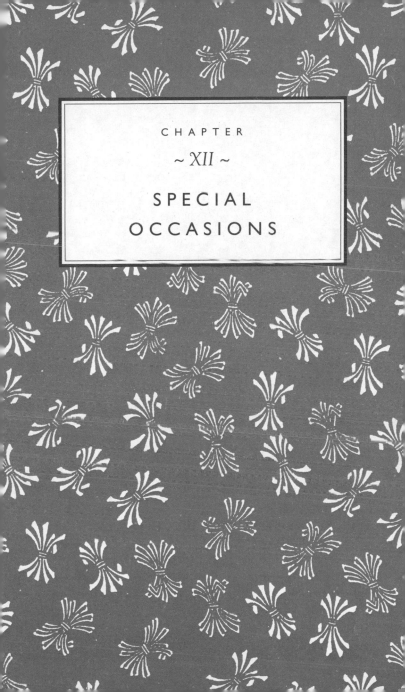

CHAPTER

~ XII ~

SPECIAL
OCCASIONS

~ TEA CEREMONIES ~

IF YOU are invited to attend a tea ceremony, be sure to inquire about the formality of the occasion. For a formal tea ceremony women should wear a one-piece dress or skirt and blouse and men should wear a suit and tie. An informal setting does not require formal clothing, but still requires a quiet manner. Whether the ceremony is formal or informal, be aware that you will be stocking-footed and be seated for a long period on tatami or perhaps *zabuton*, so avoid unnecessarily tight clothing or threadbare socks.

Each school of tea ceremony has its own rules of behavior for the host or hostess. If it is your first time, someone will either show you by example or teach you the proper manners, so you need not worry about being rude through not knowing all the movements.

In general, the guest will bow at the entrance to the room, greet the other guests with a bow, and sit down in the place indicated. First one is served a small cake (*o-kashi*) that is to be eaten in several bites. Usually you pick up the small plate that the cake is served on and hold it beneath the cake while you are eating. Take care that you do not drop crumbs.

When the tea is served, bow to the guests who have not been served, pick up the bowl in your right hand, and then hold it in both hands. Turn the bowl clockwise two quarter turns (to avoid drinking from the front of the bowl) and drink the tea in several sips.

When finished drinking, turn the bowl counterclockwise to the original position and place the bowl in front of you, just beyond the seam of the tatami. Make a formal bow to the host or hostess. If there are only a few guests remaining to be served, you may look carefully at the tea bowl to appreciate it. It is acceptable to pick up the bowl again, but hold it close to your lap. That way, if it should slip out of your hand, it will fall only a short distance. Given the extraordinary cost of some tea utensils, this is a natural precaution.

Once your turn is over, the next person will be served. Polite conversation may be made while the other guests are being served, but avoid being talkative or loud. At the completion of the ceremony everyone makes a bow of gratitude for the event, then departs.

~ EXHIBITS AND ~ RECITALS

IF A FRIEND or acquaintance is participating in an exhibition of art works or flower arrangements, you might wish to find out if and when that person will be in attendance at the exhibit and try to visit during that time. If you are specifically invited and receive admission tickets, you can show your appreciation by bringing along a friend or by taking a box of cookies as a gift of congratulations.

If you attend a performance as a guest, you might take a bouquet of flowers or a small gift such as cookies.

~ MARTIAL ARTS ~

IF YOU are invited to a martial arts practice hall (*dōjō*), you need only remember to bow as you enter the door and take off your shoes before stepping onto the matted or wooden floor. If practice is in session, stand or sit on your heels (*seiza*) along the wall. As elsewhere, men may change to sitting cross-legged and women may put their legs out to one side. You need not follow the bowing formalities of the people practicing, but if you are introduced to the teachers, bow formally.

~ BIRTHDAY PARTIES ~

JAPANESE MAY celebrate children's birthdays with a party and invitations to the child's friends. Guests bring presents and take-home favors are provided to them by the child's parents.

Adult birthdays are not marked by celebrations until later in life when families celebrate the attainment of milestones at ages sixty-one, seventy, seventy-seven, eighty-eight, and ninety-nine.

APPENDIX

~ ANNUAL EVENTS ~

January

JAPANESE FAMILIES usually spend January 1 (*gantan*) and the next two or three days reading New Year's greeting cards (*nengajō*), eating special New Year's dishes (*o-sechi ryōri*), making first visits to shrines or temples (*hatsumōde*), and entertaining a few guests and relatives in their homes. This period is an extended holiday for banks, public offices, and most companies. One makes formal first visits (*nenshi-mawari*) to superiors, usually taking a gift of food. The common greeting is *Akemashite omedetō gozaimasu. Kotoshi mo dōzo yoroshiku o-negai shimasu.*

The first day of work in the new year (*shigoto hajime*) varies from employer to employer, but generally falls on the sixth or seventh. One should ask beforehand when business resumes after the holidays. In large enterprises the first day of work is comprised of formal greetings and perhaps a short party, so real business resumes on the next weekday.

Adults' Day (*seijin no hi*), on the fifteenth, is a national holiday honoring the legal coming of age of young people who have reached twenty. Local governments hold ceremonies to recognize young people and private parties follow. Friends and relatives may present neckties, card cases, or accessories to men and necklaces, earrings, or other accessories to women.

February

February 14 is Valentine's Day, a day on which Japanese women give chocolate to the men in their lives. At their workplaces some female employees present *giri-choko*, "obligatory chocolate," to their supervisors and other male employees. There has not been such wide acceptance of the custom of men returning chocolate on "White Day," March 14.

March

The Dolls' Festival or Girls' Festival *(hina matsuri)* takes place on the third. It is essentially a family affair in which traditional dolls are displayed and special cakes and sweets are eaten by girls and their friends.

The latter half of March is graduation season. Since school years come to a close in late March, this is a time for giving gifts to graduates of the various levels of schooling.

The week centering around the day of the vernal equinox *(shumbun no hi)* in late March is called *higan* and during this time Buddhist families hold ceremonies for their ancestors and visit the family grave.

March and April mark the transfer season. Many enterprises make personnel transfers effective on or about April 1, so this is a time for expressing gratitude to those who will be moving on. One presents gifts to those to whom one has been indebted and wishes them the best in their new positions. Very often colleagues will go to the train station to see off the departing person and will present them with a bouquet. The person who is moving to a new position will send out printed postcards thanking people for their past favors and informing them of the new position and new addresses and telephone numbers.

April

April 1 is the start of a new year for many things in Japan. Every school from elementary school to university starts its year on this day, March graduates officially start their new jobs on this day, the fiscal year begins for most enterprises, and many personnel transfers become effective on this day. One gives congratulatory presents to friends and family members and to the children of those one is indebted to.

Flower viewing (*hana-mi*) also takes place at this time. When the cherry trees begin to put forth their blossoms, groups of friends, colleagues, and students take to the parks to sit under the trees and drink and eat.

April 29 is Green Day (*midori no hi*). This national holiday was formerly to honor the Showa emperor's birthday, but it now reminds us of the importance of nature and greenery. It is the commencement of the "Golden Week" of national holidays and some enterprises take the whole week off.

May

Constitution Day (*kempō kinenbi*) is on May 3. This

national holiday recalls the day in 1947 when the postwar constitution came into effect.

Children's Day *(kodomo no hi)* on May 5 is also a national holiday.

Mothers' Day *(haha no hi)* on the second Sunday of May is an occasion for children to honor their mother with a gift of red carnations and perhaps a dinner out.

June

June 1 means changing clothes *(koromo-gae)*. On this day many schools have their students and some companies have their employees change from winter uniforms to summer uniforms.

Fathers' Day *(chichi no hi)* on the third Sunday is a day children honor their fathers with gifts such as a necktie.

July

The first three weeks of July is the summer gift season *(o-chūgen)*, which is described on page 77.

During the Buddhist Festival of the Dead *(obon)*, families "welcome" the spirits of their ancestors on the thirteenth and "send them forth" on the sixteenth. During this period many people return to their parental homes and visit the graves of their ancestors. (This festival is celebrated one month later in some areas.)

August

The Buddhist Festival of the Dead *(obon)* from the

thirteenth to the sixteenth is the same as that de-scribed in July.

September

Respect for the Aged Day (*keirō no hi*) on the fifteenth is a national holiday and primarily a family observance.

The autumnal equinox (*shūbun no hi*) on the twenty-third is a national holiday. This day is the middle day of the week-long *higan* period, whose spring counterpart is observed in March.

October

Physical Culture Day (*tai-iku no hi*) on the tenth is a national holiday and peak of the *undōkai* (athletic meet) season. Day-long outdoor physical activities are held by schools, companies, and communities. One usually takes a mat to sit on and a lunch from home with food to share with others.

November

Culture Day (*bunka no hi*) on the third is a national holiday and occasion for lectures, exhibitions, and displays of cultural activities.

New Year's cards (*nengajō*) go on sale in the middle of this month. The postal service will accept addressed cards beginning in December. By the end of the month, families who are observing one year of mourning (*mochū*) for a deceased family member will send out postcards called *mochū ketsurei no aisatsu*, letting others know that they will not be mailing New Year's cards that year. Some hold that it is acceptable to mail cards to families in mourning, but the more general practice is to refrain from doing so for that year.

Labor Thanksgiving Day (*kinrō kansha no hi*) on the twenty-third is a national holiday.

December

Shiwasu, the poetic name for December, means that everyone, even teachers, are so busy that they run during this month. The reason for mentioning it here is to warn that work schedules are rather full at this time of year and few people will have the freedom to take on new tasks. It is also a season for year-end parties (*bōnenkai*) and virtually every business, association, group, committee, and club will have some kind of party. The term *bōnen* literally means "forget (the stresses and strains of) the past year."

The first three weeks of December is *o-seibo* or winter gift season. This is the second of the seasonal gift-giving seasons, for which details are given in Chapter VIII, beginning on page 75.

New Year's cards (*nengajō*) are mailed toward the end of the month. The postal service guarantees delivery early on the morning of January 1 of those cards mailed by approximately December 23.

The Emperor's Birthday (*tennō tanjōbi*) on the twenty-third is a national holiday.

Christmas Day is not a national holiday in Japan. However, in addition to the normal Christian celebrations, many Japanese have adopted Christmas Eve as a time for parties, dates, and the eating of decorated cakes.

The last week of the month marks the conclusion of work *(shigoto osame)*. As almost all public offices and enterprises come to a complete halt a few days before the end of the year to allow employees to take care of their own preparations, it is wise to inquire at important offices when they will close down and reopen for business at the beginning of January. In some cases this is a week-long holiday.

The preparations for the new year include the writing of New Year's cards, cleaning house, and preparing special dishes.

New Year's Eve *(ōmisoka)* on the thirty-first is the last-moment shopping day and in the hours before midnight the commencement of the first visits to shrines and temples for making wishes. The ringing of temple bells signals the start of the new year.

~ GLOSSARY ~

aizuchi sound or short word used to respond to what
another is saying; rejoinder

baishakunin go-between in marriage; also **nakōdo**
bushūgi-bukuro envelope for a monetary offering at
a funeral; also **kōden-bukuro**

chigai-dana staggered shelves, usually adjacent to
the *toko-no-ma*
chōden condolence telegram
chōnaikai neighborhood association

fukusa small wrapping cloth

genkan small vestibule at the entrance of a house
giri choko "obligatory chocolate" given by a woman
to a male colleague on Valentine's Day
gochisōsama deshita expression of thanks after a
meal
gokurōsama expression of thanks to a subordinate
after some service has been performed; expression
said at the end of the workday to a departing
colleague
gomen kudasai expression used when entering a
home to announce one's arrival

hikide-mono return gift to a guest from the bride
and groom at a wedding banquet
hōji Buddhist memorial service for the dead

hori-gotatsu sunken area in the floor with a table frame and heating unit covered with a quilt for warming the legs

itadakimasu expression of thanks before a meal

kaishi tissue paper

kampai "Cheers!" expression used for a toast

kata-gaki position within a company or society

kekkon hirōen wedding reception

kekkon-shiki wedding ceremony

kōden monetary offering to the deceased's family; condolence gift

kōden-bukuro envelope used for a monetary offering at a funeral; also **bushūgi-bukuro**

kokubetsu-shiki rite for bidding farewell to the deceased

kotatsu foot-warmer composed of a quilt over a table frame and heating unit

kotobuki character meaning good luck, as on a New Year's card or wedding gift

meishi name card, business card

miai kekkon arranged marriage

mizuhiki decorative wrapping cord made of twisted paper string

nakōdo go-between in marriage; also **baishakunin**

nengajō New Year's card

nenshi-mawari making the rounds to congratulate one's friends, relatives, and business associates at New Year's

noshi narrow strip of dried abalone wrapped in red

and white paper (or image thereof), used as a decoration on a present or envelope

noshi-bukuro gift envelope

o-chūgen midsummer gift to express appreciation

o-hashi chopsticks

o-ironaoshi changing of the bride's clothes during a wedding banquet

o-iwai dempō congratulatory telegram sent on a felicitous occasion like a wedding

o-jama shimasu expression used when entering a house or room

o-kaeshi return gift

o-kuyami dempō condolence telegram

o-medetō gozaimasu expression meaning congratulations

o-mimai inquiring after someone's health

o-miyage gift

omoi-yari mutual consideration

omotegaki character or characters written on a formal gift envelope

o-negai shimasu expression used when making a request

onsen hot spring

o-rei expression of appreciation

o-saki ni shitsurei shimasu expression said to one's remaining colleagues when departing the workplace

o-seibo midwinter gift to express appreciation

o-shibori small, damp towel offered to a guest for wiping the hands

o-toshidama small gift of money to a child at New Year's

o-tsukaresama expression said to a colleague as he or she leaves the office at the end of the day
o-zen raised dining tray

ren'ai kekkon love-match marriage
ryokan Japanese-style inn

sakazuki small cup for drinking saké
sentō public bathing facility
shūgi-bukuro envelope for a monetary gift on a felicitous occasion like a wedding
sōgi funeral service

tenugui long washcloth
tokkuri small flask for warming and serving saké
toko-no-ma recessed alcove
tsuya wake

uchi-iwai small present given on the occasion of a family celebration

yaku-doshi year traditionally held to be inauspicious or critical
yoroshiku (o-negai shimasu) expression used to make a request
yukata informal cotton kimono worn in summer and in *ryokan* when going to and from the bath

zabuton square floor cushion